Purchasing Power

HARNESSING INSTITUTIONAL PROCUREMENT
FOR PEOPLE AND THE PLANET

LISA MASTNY

Thomas Prugh, *Editor*

WORLDWATCH PAPER 166

July 2003

THE WORLDWATCH INSTITUTE is an independent research organization that works for an environmentally sustainable and socially just society, in which the needs of all people are met without threatening the health of the natural environment or the well-being of future generations. By providing compelling, accessible, and fact-based analysis of critical global issues, Worldwatch informs people around the world about the complex interactions among people, nature, and economies. Worldwatch focuses on the underlying causes of and practical solutions to the world's problems, in order to inspire people to demand new policies, investment patterns, and lifestyle choices.

FINANCIAL SUPPORT for the Institute is provided by the Aria Foundation, the Richard & Rhoda Goldman Fund, The George Gund Foundation, The William and Flora Hewlett Foundation, The Frances Lear Foundation, The John D. and Catherine T. MacArthur Foundation, the Merck Family Fund, the Curtis and Edith Munson Foundation, Nalith, Inc., the NIB Foundation, The Overbrook Foundation, The David and Lucile Packard Foundation, The Shared Earth Foundation, The Shenandoah Foundation, Turner Foundation, Inc., the UN Environment Programme, the Wallace Global Fund, the Weeden Foundation, and The Winslow Foundation. The Institute also receives financial support from its Council of Sponsors members Adam and Rachel Albright, Tom and Cathy Crain, John and Laurie McBride and Kate McBride Puckett, Robert Wallace and Raisa Scriabine, and from the many other friends of Worldwatch.

THE WORLDWATCH PAPERS provide in-depth, quantitative, and qualitative analysis of the major issues affecting prospects for a sustainable society. The Papers are written by members of the Worldwatch Institute research staff or outside specialists and are reviewed by experts unaffiliated with Worldwatch. They have been used as concise and authoritative references by governments, nongovernmental organizations, and educational institutions worldwide. For a partial list of available Worldwatch Papers, go online to www.worldwatch.org/pubs/paper.

The views expressed are those of the author and do not necessarily represent those of the Worldwatch Institute; of its directors, officers, or staff; or of its funding organizations.

Contents

Acknowledgments: Many thanks to Scot Case, Chad Dobson, and Arthur Weissman for their helpful comments on earlier drafts of this paper. Thanks also to Julia Schreiner Alves, Shelley Billik, Dominique Brief, Patricia Brink, Owen Davis, Marcia Deegler, Matt DeLuca, Holly Elwood, Tom Ferguson, Anne-Francoise Gailly, Gerard Gleason, Dean Kubani, Berny Letreille, Mike Liles, Michael Marx, Luz Aída Martínez Meléndez, Maureen Moore, Keith Robinson, Hiroyuki Sato, Tom Snyder, Maria Vargas, and John Zurcher for their valuable insights on specific sections and their kind help with data and information.

I also appreciate the support from my colleagues at Worldwatch. Editor Tom Prugh helped me finesse the language and structure of the paper, while Hilary French, Gary Gardner, and Brian Halweil provided thoughtful comments on early drafts. Clayton Adams doggedly pursued elusive facts and meticulously checked the data and sources to ensure that the paper came together. Dani Nierenberg and Steve Conklin provided much-needed moral support during the project, and Art Director Lyle Rosbotham magically transformed the text and figures. And Leanne Mitchell and Susan Finkelpearl helped to hone and communicate the message.

I owe special thanks to my parents, Catherine Mastny-Fox and Vojtech Mastny, for showing me the possibilities of a better world.

Finally, I would like to extend my appreciation to the Merck Family Fund and the Overbrook Foundation, whose support has been so important to the success of this effort.

Lisa Mastny is a research associate at the Worldwatch Institute, where she covers a wide range of environment and development topics. She is the author of Worldwatch Paper 159, *Traveling Light: New Paths for International Tourism* (December 2001), and a contributing author of the Institute's annual books, *State of the World* and *Vital Signs*. She has also written for *World Watch* magazine on topics ranging from ecotourism to environmental change in the Arctic. Lisa holds master's degrees in international relations and environmental studies from Yale University and a bachelor's degree in international studies from Johns Hopkins University.

SUMMARY

Through their purchases, governments, corporations, universities, and other large institutions wield great influence over the future of our planet. Nearly every purchase an institution makes, from office paper to buildings, has hidden costs for the natural environment and the world's people.

Shifting just a portion of institutional spending away from harmful goods and services to more environmentally friendly alternatives can benefit ecosystems and communities around the world as well as save money. Green purchasing can also send a powerful message to the market, showing manufacturers that institutional consumers of all kinds increasingly demand more sustainable options.

Around the world, growing numbers of forward-thinking institutions are reviewing their purchasing habits and incorporating environmental concerns into all stages of their procurements. These pioneering organizations are minimizing their planetary environmental footprints, in many cases also improving their bottom lines, and serving as successful models for other institutions.

But there's still a long way to go. Worldwide, this movement remains relatively small-scale, scattered, and ill-defined. Current activity is largely restricted to industrial countries and has yet to spread meaningfully to institutions in much of the developing world. And even within industrial countries, few organizations realize the tremendous potential of their purchasing to effect positive environmental change.

Spreading the movement won't be easy. Today's institu-

tions face many political, legal, institutional, and other hurdles that prevent them from effectively harnessing this potential. Among these hurdles are internal resistance from managers
reluctant to alter time-honored purchasing practices, potential
barriers from international trade regimes as well as other legal
obstacles, and opposition from producers of conventional
goods and services, which could lose out in the transition to
a more sustainable world.

Although not a panacea, harnessing institutional purchasing may be one of the most powerful tools available for
shifting patterns of production and consumption in a more
sustainable direction. We need to learn how we can push these
organizations to respond to the rising demands for a more
sustainable world.

Introduction

"**W**ANTED for Victory: waste paper, old rags, scrap metals, old rubber."[1]* In the early 1940s, at the peak of the Second World War, colorful posters with messages like this adorned building facades and lampposts across the United States. Commissioned by the federal government, they urged citizens to ration paper and metal, grow their own food, join car-sharing clubs, and make other sacrifices for the war effort. At a time of heightened global instability, resource conservation was the order of the day.

How things have changed. More than half a century later, following the terrorist attacks of September 2001, one of the strongest messages the Bush administration sent to the American public was not to economize but to consume.[2] By buying new cars, houses, and other goods, consumers could do their part to boost the flagging U.S. economy. The way to minimize the domestic impacts of rising global insecurity was not to conserve energy and other resources, but to use even more of them.

The U.S. government is riding a powerful wave. The United Nations reports that global consumption spending has increased six-fold since 1950, reaching $24 trillion in 1998.[3] As the demand for goods and services grows, manufacturers are pumping out an ever more varied array of products. Each year, some 50,000 new consumer items are introduced in the United States, compared with only a few

---

* Endnotes are grouped by section and begin on page 54.

thousand annually in 1970.[4] Worldwide, the Organisation
for Economic Co-operation and Development predicts that as
many as half of the products that will be on the market in the
next 10 to 15 years don't even exist today.[5]

Although this production has brought improvements in
health care, sanitation, and other areas, it has also come at great
cost. Nearly every item we buy, from cars to bananas, has
hidden impacts on the natural environment or on human welfare.[6] Obtaining enough gold for a single 14-carat wedding ring,
weighing just one-tenth of an ounce, involves digging up as
many as three tons of waste rock and ore, and can have dev-
astating effects on ecosystems and communities living near
mining operations.[7] Many of the products we rely on require
huge inputs of water, wood, energy, metals, and other resources
that are not always renewable. And they often contain toxic
chemicals that, when released into the environment, endan-
ger the health of humans and the ecological systems we
depend on. These impacts can occur at any stage of a product's
life: obtaining the raw materials, manufacturing, packaging and
transport, use, and even after disposal.

Responsibility for this resource use is not shared equally.
According to the United Nations, the wealthiest one-fifth of
the world's population now owns 87 percent of all cars and con-
sumes 84 percent of all paper, 65 percent of all electricity,
and 45 percent of all meat and fish.[8] (This global consumer class
includes not just the majority of people in industrial countries,
but also a growing minority in the developing world.) In con-
trast, another one-fifth of humanity—approximately 1.3 billion people worldwide—continues to live on less than $1 a day
per person, unable to consume enough to meet basic requirements for food, shelter, and energy.[9]

These global consumption patterns almost certainly can-
not be sustained. As world population and the demand for
goods and services continue to soar—and as more people in
developing countries seek to emulate Western lifestyles—pressures on the global environment will only intensify.[10] The average world citizen already uses resources at a rate higher than
the Earth's biologically available capacity to replenish them,

according to estimates by the California-based group Redefining Progress.[11]* (See Figure 1.) If everyone in the world consumed like the average U.S. citizen, we would need at least four more planet Earths.

FIGURE 1

Number of Earths Needed If Everyone Consumed Like...

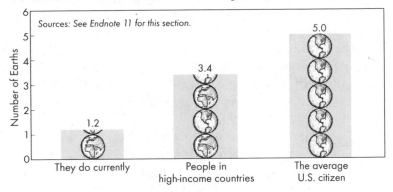

Sources: See Endnote 11 for this section.

Number of Earths

- They do currently — 1.2
- People in high-income countries — 3.4
- The average U.S. citizen — 5.0

Addressing today's unsustainable patterns of production and consumption is one of the most difficult challenges of the 21st century. In addition to aggressive strategies to boost the standard of living of the world's poor, this will require significant changes in both the scale and efficiency of resource use. Manufacturers will need to rethink the way they design and make products in order to minimize the negative impacts of their production on the planet. And consumers, particularly in industrial countries, will need to reexamine their buying practices, considering less wasteful and more environmentally sound ways to satisfy their needs.

One part of the solution is "green purchasing," that is, shifting spending away from goods and services that cause environmental and social harm, and toward products that are more environmentally sound and socially just. These include products that conserve energy and resources, generate less

---

* Calculations are based on the biologically productive area needed to produce the resources used and absorb the waste generated by the population, per Redefining Progress, *Ecological Footprint Accounts: Moving Sustainability from Concept to Measurable Goal* (Oakland, CA: 2002).

waste and pollution, and are less toxic to human and environmental health. Although buying green isn't the only way to reduce the hidden costs of our consumption (green purchasing is, after all, still a form of consumption), it is an important step.

Consumer demand can play an important role in building markets for environmentally preferable goods and services. If consumers increasingly seek out products and services that are more beneficial to the environment, producers will have a greater incentive to design and produce them. As markets for these items grow, propelled by the forces of competition and innovation, the resulting economies of scale will eventually drive down prices, making greener purchases more affordable for everyone.

This is not a pipe dream. Already, markets for a wide range of environmentally preferable products are growing rapidly. Global sales of energy-efficient compact fluorescent lamps have increased nearly 13-fold since 1990, to some 606 million units in 2001.[12] Use of solar energy and wind power has surged by more than 30 percent annually over the past five years in countries like Japan, Germany, and Spain.[13] Retail sales of organic produce in the United States have grown by at least 20 percent annually since 1990, to $10 billion per year, while U.S. sales of hybrid-electric cars doubled in 2001.[14]

Even so, green markets are tiny relative to the size of conventional ones. The U.S.-based Natural Marketing Institute estimates that the global demand for "health and sustainability" products, from alternative transport to organic foods, reached a record $546 billion in 2000.[15] But this still represents only about 1 percent of the total world economy.[16]

Even in industrial countries, markets for many green products struggle to remain viable. For instance, despite extensive efforts to boost the market share of recycled paper in the United States, an estimated 95 percent of the country's printing and writing grade paper (which accounts for more than a quarter of the U.S. paper market) is still made from virgin wood fiber.[17] Domestic use of recycled paper has actually declined in recent years, notes Gerard Gleason, associate direc-

THE POWER OF PROCUREMENT

tor of the U.S. non-profit Conservatree. He warns that unless demand picks up, the infrastructure for manufacturing it could soon disappear.

Green markets in the developing world are even smaller, though interest in renewable energy and other product areas is growing.[18] Although overall resource use in these countries is still low relative to the industrial world, rising consumer demand will make strengthening local markets for environmentally sound technologies increasingly important.

Addressing today's consumption challenges will require commitment from all areas of society. Producers, consumers, individuals, and institutions all need to recognize the connection between the things we buy and environmental and social justice. One important place to start is by harnessing the power of institutional procurement.*

The Power of Procurement

The world's institutions are significant consumers, spending enormous sums on goods and services to help them run efficiently and achieve their missions. These purchases range from durable goods like office equipment and fleet vehicles to important services like electric power, custodial cleaning, and catering.

Because of both the scale of their buying and the visibility of their activities, institutions are important players in the movement to build more sustainable markets. Diverting even a small portion of institutional spending to more environmentally sound products and services can send a powerful message to the marketplace. It can also reduce the overall footprint of institutional consumption, bringing widespread environmental and economic benefits.

Just how powerful is institutional purchasing? Consider

---

* A distinction is sometimes made between purchasing (buying products and materials for operational use) and procurement (buying parts and materials as inputs into manufactured products). In this paper, however, the terms are used interchangeably.

governments. In industrial countries, public purchasing accounts for as much as 25 percent of gross domestic product (GDP).[1]* (See Figure 2.) Government procurement in the European Union alone totaled more than $1 trillion in 2001, or roughly 14 percent of GDP.[2] In North America, it reached $2 trillion, or about 18 percent of regional GDP.[3] This purchasing occurs at all levels of government: in 2002, the United States federal government spent roughly $350 billion on goods and services (excluding military spending), while the country's state and local authorities spent more than $400 billion.[4]

Corporations, universities, religious bodies, and other large institutions also have significant purchasing power. Many businesses, for instance, not only buy myriad finished products, such as pens and computers, but also raw materials, packaging, and other goods as inputs into the manufacturing process. This purchasing often occurs along lengthy supply chains that span the globe: Adidas-Salomon, a leading German sporting goods manufacturer, now relies on some 828 factories worldwide, more than half of which are in Asia.[5] By one estimate, aggregate spending by companies along their supply chains far outweighs the consumption of finished products by individuals.[6] As production becomes ever more global, manufacturers can play an important role in influencing the environmental behavior of their suppliers in other countries, including in the developing world.

Meanwhile, universities spend billions of dollars each year on everything from campus buildings to cafeteria food. The roughly 3,700 colleges and universities in the United States collectively bought some $250 billion in goods and services in 1999—equivalent to nearly 3 percent of U.S. GDP, and more than the GDP of any country but the world's 18 largest.[7] Religious institutions have similar clout, managing vast numbers of schools and houses of worship around the world, as well as wielding significant influence over the behavior of their adherents.[8]

International institutions like the United Nations, the

---

* Up to three-quarters of this spending goes for purchases of consumable goods and services, while the remainder goes to capital goods and investment spending.

FIGURE 2

Government Spending as Share of GDP, Selected Countries, 1998

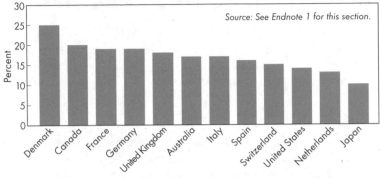

Source: See Endnote 1 for this section.

World Bank, and other multilateral players are also big spenders. They buy large quantities of goods and services, not only to run their headquarters and operations in industrial countries but also to sustain their field offices and activities in the developing world—giving them a unique opportunity to help build sustainable markets in these countries. The United Nations alone bought nearly $4 billion worth of goods and services in 2000.[9]

But the sheer volume of their purchasing is only one reason institutions can be powerful agents for positive environmental change. "Unlike many individuals, large institutions take a very systematic approach to their purchasing," notes Scot Case of the Maryland-based Center for a New American Dream. "Purchases are clearly defined in detailed contracts that specify nearly every aspect of the product or service being bought."[10] With structured methodologies already in place, inserting environmental considerations into institutional purchasing can be a relatively straightforward process with significant pay-offs.

For many common institutional purchases, alternatives now exist that are less resource intensive, less polluting, and less harmful to human and environmental health than their conventional counterparts.[11] (See Sidebar 1, pp. 14–17.) For instance, by buying paper with even a small percentage of recycled content, institutions can divert significant amounts of waste from landfills and stimulate wider markets for recycled goods.[12] They can also save energy, wood, and other resources:

SIDEBAR 1

Common Institutional Purchases:
Environmental Impacts and Greener Alternatives

Purchase	Impacts	Greener Alternatives
Building construction, renovation, use	Worldwide, construction and use consume 40 percent of raw stone, gravel, and sand; 25 percent of virgin wood; and a large share of water. Buildings require energy to heat, light, power, and cool, and can account for the highest share of an institution's climate-altering greenhouse gas (GHG) emissions. Materials and furnishings can contain toxins that endanger human and ecosystem health.	Energy-efficient cements, windows, heating and cooling units. Natural lighting and power from renewable sources like passive solar. Use of certified wood and materials with low toxicity and cleaning needs and with recycled content. Non-polyvinyl chloride (PVC) piping, cables, and windows.
Electricity (coal, oil, natural gas)	Emissions from fossil fuel combustion during power generation and transmission contribute to climate change and acid precipitation. Coal has the highest GHG emissions, followed by oil and natural gas.	Renewables like solar, wind, and tidal power that displace generation from fossil fuels.
Paper	Producing 1 ton of virgin office paper requires 6.5 tons of wood and produces 2.8 tons of GHGs and over a ton of solid waste. Wood use causes deforestation and biodiversity loss. Chlorine from bleaching can contaminate water and accumulate in living tissue. Each year, U.S. office workers discard some 12 million tons of paper.	Paper with high post-consumer recycled content. (Recycled content uses fewer chemicals than virgin pulping and releases up to 36 percent fewer GHGs.) Paper from sustainably managed forests, sawdust, or scrap. Non-bleached or chlorine-free bleached paper.
Lighting	GHG emissions from electricity consumption contribute to	Energy efficient compact fluorescent lamps.

Sidebar 1 (continued)

	climate change. Mercury emissions during product use and disposal.	Lamps with low mercury content and with electronic, not magnetic, ballasts. Motion sensors and timers.
Carpets/ flooring	Processing, manufacturing, and transport are energy intensive. In North America, 95 percent of carpet backings are petroleum based. Raw materials and surface treatments contain PVC and other toxins that affect indoor air quality and contaminate after disposal. Cleaning can release toxins.	Individual carpet tiles that are durable and replaceable. Natural carpet fibers. Woods from sustainable forests. Products with minimum cleaning requirements, PVC content, and emissions. Non-toxic surface treatments.
Vehicles/ personal transport	Every liter of gasoline burned emits some 2.5 kilograms of GHGs. NOx and VOCs contribute to ground level ozone and smog formation. Emissions are rising due to increased vehicle use globally and declining fuel-efficiencies in North America.	Vehicles with high fuel economy and low emissions. Alternatives like electric, hybrid-electric, clean natural gas. Using the most appropriate vehicle, public transport, car sharing, or bicycles.
Office furniture	Uses wood, metals, and other resources. Plastics contain PVC or phthalates; paints and lacquers contain carcinogenic dyes. Heavy metals, VOCs, and other toxins released during manufacturing and from surface treatments.	High quality, durable, and repairable furniture. Wood from sustainably harvested forests. Surfaces that are untreated or treated with linseed, soap, wax, or water-based alternatives.
IT equipment (PCs, printers, phones, fax machines, copiers)	Making a typical desktop computer creates 63 kilograms of waste and 22 kilograms of hazardous materials. Computers and monitors use up to 7	Energy-efficient computers with power-down modes, which can cut electricity costs of office equip-

16

Sidebar 1 (continued)

percent of commercial electricity and release between 32 and 1,317 kilograms of CO_2 equivalent per year, depending on model. Also release persistent, toxic, and bioaccumulative heavy metals after disposal.

ment by half. Machines with replaceable modular components or with guaranteed manufacturer take-back policies. Copiers and printers with two-sided printing.

Cleaning products

Can contain toxic chemicals linked with cancer, reproductive and respiratory ailments, and other health issues, causing high janitorial turnover. Toxins also affect water quality and plant and animal health.

Products that are biodegradable, low in VOCs, and free of carcinogens and phosphates.

Coffee makers

Impacts depend on model, accessories, and use. The average pot brews in 12 minutes but stays on the burner for 3 hours. Energy use ranges from 41 to 774 kilograms of CO_2 equivalent. Paper filters contribute to landfill waste. Also impacts associated with coffee growing, picking, roasting, and transport.

Insulated thermal carafes that require no electricity beyond the brewing time. Metal filters that can be washed and reused. Shade-grown or fair-trade certified coffee.

Cafeteria foods

High pesticide and fertilizer use causes nitrification, acidification, toxicity of water and soil. Conversion of forests to crop and ranchland contributes to biodiversity loss, soil erosion. Methane emissions from livestock contribute to climate change. Food processing and transport are often energy-intensive. Packaging impacts.

Locally grown and produced foods. Higher share of organic content. Skipping one beef meal a week saves 32 kilograms of grain, 32 kilograms of topsoil, and 151,400 liters of water. Food with biodegradable, recyclable, or no packaging.

Pest management

Chemicals in pesticides can contaminate soil and ground-

Integrated pest management that uses

Sidebar 1 (continued)

water, bioaccumulate in the food chain, and affect human and ecosystem health. An estimated 90 percent of the product doesn't reach the intended target.

non-toxic or less-toxic products. Removing weeds manually or mechanically. Using natural biological deterrents.

Sources: See Endnote 11 for this section.

the New York-based environmental group Environmental Defense estimates that if the entire U.S. catalog industry switched its publications to just 10 percent recycled content paper, the savings in wood alone would be enough to stretch a 1.8 meter-high fence across the United States seven times.[13]

Buying greener products can also bring health benefits to employees and other building occupants. Many common institutional purchases, including paints used on walls and furniture, pesticides for buildings and grounds maintenance, and products for custodial cleaning, contain toxic ingredients like heavy metals and volatile organic compounds. These substances can pollute indoor air and accumulate in living tissue, endangering human and environmental health. The Janitorial Products Pollution Prevention Project reports that 6 out of every 100 janitors in the U.S. state of Washington have lost time from their jobs as a result of injuries related to the use of toxic cleaning products, particularly glass and toilet cleaners and degreasers.[14]

Many institutions are finding that green purchasing not only brings environmental savings but can also save money.[15] Recycled paper, for instance, now costs the same as or less than virgin paper in many European countries.[16]* Municipal purchasers in Dunkerque, France, have found that they now save about $.50 per ream (about 16 percent) by buying recycled.[17]

---

* In the United States, however, buyers generally still pay a premium of 4 to 8 percent for recycled content paper, per Gerard Gleason, associate director of Conservatree, San Francisco, discussion with Clayton Adams, Worldwatch Institute, 7 April 2003.

This shows, as is the case with many new technologies, that green products often cost more at first because they have innovative features that are expensive to develop, or because markets for them are too small to benefit from economies of scale.[18] But as these markets grow, many will become increasingly cost-competitive with conventional items.

Some green products are simply cheaper than their conventional alternatives. Recycled toner cartridges for printers and copiers, for instance, can sell for a third the price of new cartridges. Other items, such as compact fluorescent lamps (CFLs) or low-flush toilets, bring considerable cost savings over their lifetimes. Although CFLs cost up to 20 times more than incandescent bulbs, they last 10 times longer and use a quarter of the electricity to produce the same amount of light.[19] Buying goods that are durable, remanufactured, and/or recyclable can lower the costs of product maintenance, replacement, or disposal. Meanwhile, cleaners and other products that are less toxic can reduce the insurance and worker's compensation expenses associated with certain workplace injuries.[20]

Green Purchasing Pioneers

As the benefits of green purchasing become increasingly apparent, many institutions are beginning to reexamine their buying habits and adopt more environmentally sound policies and practices. Most of these pioneers are targeting "low-hanging-fruit" purchases, like paper and office supplies, that are easy to shift without significant changes in the organization's practices. But some have begun to fundamentally restructure the way they do business.

At the corporate level, green purchasing pioneers include companies in virtually all sectors of the economy, including banks, hotels, automakers, clothing retailers, and supermarkets.[1] (See Sidebar 2.) Many of these businesses are motivated by enlightened self-interest: they are finding that by embracing energy efficiency measures and other relatively small-scale

Examples of Green Purchasing in Selected Companies

Bank of America
Boosted recycled paper purchases by 11 percent in 2001, to 54 percent of paper bought. Reuses and refurbishes office furniture and carpeting and uses recycled materials in fixtures and bank service counters. Aims to include supplier environmental requirements in all future contracts.

Boeing
By 1999, had retrofitted more than half of its floor space with efficient lighting, cutting energy costs by $12 million annually and saving enough energy to power some 16,000 homes.

Canon
Gives priority in its global purchasing to nearly 4,600 company-approved green office supplies. Now working to green its procurement for plants in Japan, Asia, and North America. Outreach to suppliers has led to high rates of compliance with existing policies.

Federal Express
In 2002, pledged to replace all 44,000 fleet vehicles with diesel-electric trucks that would increase fuel efficiency by half and cut smog- and soot-causing emissions by 90 percent.

Hewlett-Packard
In 1999, committed to buying only paper from sustainable forest sources. Gives preference to suppliers that provide green products and have green business practices. Restricts or prohibits use of certain chemicals in manufacturing and packaging.

IKEA
Gives preference to wood from forests that are either certified as being sustainably managed or transitioning to these standards. Buys wood via a four-step process that encourages suppliers to seek forest certification.

McDonald's
Spent more than $3 billion on recycled content purchases between 1990 and 1999, including trays, tables, carpeting, and packaging. In 2001, adopted compostable food packaging made from reclaimed potato starch and other materials. Has installed energy efficient lighting in restaurants.

Migros
In 2002, the Swiss supermarket became the first European retailer to stop buying palm oil supplies from ecologically unsound sources in Malaysia and Indonesia. Audits its suppliers for compliance with environmental criteria and labels products that "protect tropical forests."

Sidebar 2 (continued)

Patagonia

In 1996, switched its entire sportswear line to 100 percent organic cotton, after an extensive process of sourcing the material, educating employees, and working with suppliers and distributors.

Riu Hotels

By switching to bulk purchases of breakfast items, the German chain was able to cut waste by 5,100 kilograms annually, saving 24 million items of individual packaging and an average of five million plastic garbage bags each year.

Staples

In 2002, pledged to boost the average recycled content in its paper goods to 30 percent and to phase out purchases from endangered forests. Uses energy-efficient lighting and roofing material in its buildings. By end of 2003, aims to buy only recycled paper products for internal operations and to boost green power purchases to 5 percent.

Starbucks

Since November 2001, has offered financial incentives and supplier preference to farmers who meet certain environmental, social, economic, and quality standards. In 2002, 28 percent of paper fiber used was post-consumer and 49 percent contained unbleached fiber.

Toyota

In 2001, switched some 1,400 office supply items and 300 computers and other equipment to green alternatives. Achieved 100 percent green purchasing in these areas in 2002. Bought 500,000 kilowatthours of wind power in fiscal year 2001, and aims to boost this to 2 million kilowatthours per year.

Warner Brothers

Buys recycled content building and construction materials, office paper and supplies, and parking bumpers. Has adopted a green building standard for interior remodels. Energy efficient retrofits, including lighting, occupancy sensors, and solar electric systems, saved the company more than 4 million kilowatthours of electricity in 2002.

Sources: See Endnote 1 for this section.

changes in their internal operations, they can reduce their environmental impacts as well as improve their profitability. L'Oreal, the world's largest cosmetics manufacturer, cut its greenhouse gas emissions 40 percent between 1990 and 2000 while increasing production 60 percent, largely by installing energy efficient lighting in its facilities and introducing a recycling program to cut back on waste incineration.[2] Anheuser-Busch and IBM are among many other companies that have saved millions through improvements in water and energy efficiency.[3]

Even in cases where green purchasing doesn't lead to direct savings, it can bring overall business benefits. In a recent study for the Center for Advanced Purchasing Studies, researchers Craig R. Carter and Marianne M. Jennings found that increased corporate social responsibility is generally correlated with higher revenues, healthier and safer work environments, and improved relationships with customers and suppliers—factors that can more than outweigh any potential monetary costs.[4]

Many companies also realize that they may lose competitiveness by pursuing resource-intensive or environmentally destructive methods.[5] The sportswear manufacturer Nike, for instance, has boosted the organic cotton content of its clothing because it worries about the potential health and environmental liabilities associated with conventional cotton production, which requires high inputs of chemical pesticides and fertilizers. "It's the only intelligent way to do business," says Heidi McCloskey, global sustainability director at Nike Apparel. "By managing and designing out every harmful product, Nike won't be at risk of paying higher costs in the future."[6] In 2001, more than a third of the cotton garments the company produced contained a minimum of 3 percent certified organic cotton.[7]

Nike is in the vanguard of companies that now hope to take a leading role in pushing wider markets for green products. In 2001, it helped launch Organic Exchange, a network of 55 businesses that intends to significantly expand the use of organic cotton in manufacturing over the next 10 years.[8] Other companies, including Texas Instruments, Levi Strauss, and Ford Motor Company, have joined the industry-led Recycled Paper Coalition, founded in 1992 to use bulk corporate purchasing power to boost the supply and quality of recycled paper products (and to wean companies off virgin paper before regulations eventually require it). The coalition's 270 members bought a total of 160,000 tons of recycled paper in 2001, with an average postconsumer content of 29 percent.[9]

But balancing green purchasing with the corporate profit motive can be a delicate process. Because companies are ultimately responsible to their bottom lines and beholden to shareholder and supplier relationships, in some cases it can still be a competitive *dis*advantage to do the right thing. Jeffrey Hollender, CEO of Seventh Generation, a manufacturer of environmentally sound household goods, notes that his company is constantly weighing the urge to boost the recycled content of its products against the higher cost of doing so. "At the final analysis, it's far better to make a slightly less environmentally benign product for a time than it is to find yourself out of business and unable to make any difference at all," Hollender says. The trick is achieving a balance between moving too fast and not moving fast enough."[10]

Governments are also becoming active players in the green purchasing movement, again mainly in the industrial world. Over the past decade or so, calls for greening public procurement have escalated at the international level.[11] Most recently, delegates attending the 2002 World Summit on Sustainable Development in Johannesburg reiterated the need to "[p]romote public procurement policies that encourage development and diffusion of environmentally sound goods and services."[12] Governments also increasingly recognize the value of greening operations as a way to streamline costs and achieve wider environmental policy goals, such as reducing waste and meeting targets for energy efficiency.[13]

Although some governments took steps to green their purchasing as early as 20 years ago, most activity only dates from the early 1990s.[14] (See Sidebar 3.) Several countries—including Austria, Canada, Denmark, Germany, Japan, and the United States—now have strict national laws or policies requiring government agencies to buy green (though this doesn't mean they are always doing it; see "Overcoming Obstacles," page 29). In most other countries where green purchasing now occurs,

SIDEBAR 3

Examples of Government Green Purchasing

Australia
All governments have endorsed the 1996 National Government Waste Reduction and Purchasing Guidelines, which encourage them to buy recycled products. Procurement policy requires purchasers to take into account all relevant environmental criteria, policies, programs, costs, and benefits when formulating purchasing requirements, specifications, and requests for bids.

Austria
Local-level activities date to the late 1980s. Federal laws from 1990 and 1993 require public authorities to insert environmental criteria in product specifications. (The 1993 law has been adopted by eight of nine provinces.) Since 1997, the Ministry of Environment has helped municipalities and other ministries buy green. In 1998, the government approved basic green buying guidelines in areas like office equipment, building, cleaning, and energy.

Canada
A strong national legislative and policy framework for green purchasing exists. Goals include making 20 percent of federal power purchases from green sources by 2005 and, where cost effective and operationally feasible, running 75 percent of federal vehicles on alternative fuels by April 2004. Environment Canada's policy directs purchasers to consider product life-cycle impacts, to use ecolabeled products, and to adopt recycled, energy-efficiency, and other green criteria when purchasing.

Denmark
A world leader in green purchasing. A 1994 law requires all national and local authorities to use recycled or recyclable products, and all authorities must also have a green purchasing policy. As of 2000, 10 of 14 counties had policies. At least half of all municipalities also attest to having or developing policies.

Germany
Federal waste law requires public institutions to give preference to green products in purchasing. State and municipal directives also require inclusion of environmental criteria in requests for bids, though economic criteria take priority in evaluation.

Japan
Another world leader in green purchasing, starting with local government activity in the early 1990s. A 2001 law requires national and local governmental organizations to develop policies and buy speci-

fied green products. As of early 2003, authorities in 47 prefectures and 12 major municipalities were buying green, and nearly half the 700 municipalities had policies. Most progress is in the areas of paper, office supplies, IT equipment, cars, and home appliances.

Netherlands
Has supported green purchasing in theory since 1990, but a lack of commitment and green product information hindered early implementation. A more recent non-binding memorandum from 1996 recommends inclusion of environmental criteria in purchasing and offers stronger incentives for compliance. A new website contains information on green products and targeted activities.

Sweden
Municipalities and counties started greening their procurement in 1990. National rules advise (but do not require) public authorities to weigh environmental criteria equally when evaluating bids. More than 1,200 public and private institutions rely on green guidelines for some 25 product groups.

Switzerland
Green purchasing occurs largely on an ad-hoc basis, with groups of officials and purchasers from the federal, canton, and municipal levels sharing and exchanging information about best practices.

United Kingdom
Rules allow purchasers to use environmental criteria in purchasing as long as this doesn't prevent fair competition. Authorities can choose how much weight will be given to environmental and other criteria when awarding contracts. Government departments were required to obtain at least 5 percent of their energy from renewable sources by March 2003, and must increase this share to 10 percent by 2008.

United States
A wide array of laws and policy directives requires federal agencies to buy green items, including recycled content- and energy-efficient products and alternatively fueled vehicles. Agency-wide coordination and implementation has been poor but is improving. Among the states, 47 of 50 boast "buy-recycled" policies, some dating to the late 1980s. At least a dozen states have broadened these to include other green purchases.

Sources: See Endnote 14 for this section.

either policies "recommend" that purchasers consider environmentally preferable options, or no specific policy exists, yet purchasers are able to consider environmental variables in their buying.[15] As at the industry level, most government activity has focused on buying recycled or energy efficient products, through interest in renewable energy and other green purchases is rising as well.

There has also been a flurry of green purchasing at the local level, including among city, state, and regional governments. Christoph Erdmenger, coordinator of eco-procurement activities at the International Council for Local Environmental Initiatives (ICLEI), notes that in most countries with strong green purchasing activities, local authorities have been the forerunners.[16] In Europe, 250 municipal leaders from 36 countries pledged in the Hannover Call of 2000 to use their purchasing power "to direct development toward socially and environmentally sound solutions."[17] One leading city (Kolding, Denmark) set an ambitious goal in 1998 of incorporating environmental considerations into 100 percent of its framework purchasing by 2002. By May 2001, roughly 70 percent of its purchasing requests had specified and integrated environmental demands, primarily in the areas of food, office equipment, cleaning products, IT equipment, and health care supplies.[18]

The United States has seen greater progress in greening government purchases at the state, county, and city levels than at the national level.[19] In 1999, Santa Monica, California, became the first U.S. city to buy 100 percent of its municipal power from renewable sources, including geothermal and wind energy.[20] The state of Minnesota now has some 110 different contracts for green products and services, including alternatively fueled vehicles, low-toxicity cleaning supplies, energy-efficient computers, and solvent-free paint. Other local pioneers include the states of Massachusetts, Vermont, and Oregon; the city of Seattle, Washington; and Kalamazoo County in Michigan.[21]

In the developing world, Taiwan is one of a few countries that have formalized green public purchasing, stating a preference for approved green products in a 1998 presidential decree.[22] Other governments have implemented legislation to support recycling programs, yet initiatives to actively promote and buy recycled products have been slower to take off.[23] There has been talk about getting green purchasing into government policy in Brazil, Iran, Mexico, and Thailand, and the government of Mauritius is moving towards greater use of recycled plastic and paper and has introduced more efficient neon bulbs for street lighting.[24]

In most cases, it is too early to judge the overall impacts of government green purchasing. A few notable successes, however, point to its tremendous power to influence markets. For instance, recycled paper has become a standard office supply in many European countries, and ICLEI attributes this to the cumulative demands of public authorities, which have given the paper a competitive edge.[25] A similar shift happened when the U.S. government boosted the recycled content standard for federal paper purchases to 30 percent in 1998. In 1994, only 12 percent of the copier paper bought by federal agencies had recycled content, and this represented only 10 percent recycled material. By 2000, however, 90 percent of the paper purchased by the government's two leading paper buyers had 30 percent recycled content.[26] The spike in government demand not only boosted the overall market standard for recycled content, but also helped stabilize prices and elevate the standing of the government's main recycled paper supplier, Great White.[27]

Government green purchasing can be particularly effective in pushing markets where public buying accounts for a significant share of overall demand or where a technology is changing rapidly, as in the case of computer equipment.[28] The U.S. government, the world's single largest computer purchaser, buys more than 1 million machines annually, or roughly 7 percent of new computers worldwide.[29] In 1993, President Bill Clinton issued an executive order requiring federal agencies to buy only computer equipment that meets the efficiency requirements described under the government's Energy Star program.[30] Today, largely as a result of this increased demand, 95 percent of all monitors, 80 percent of computers, and 99 percent of printers sold in North America meet Energy Star standards.[31]* (Analysts have linked a similar jump in the environmental performance of Japanese electronics to that country's preeminence in the green purchasing of these items.)[32]

Pressures and Drivers

I nstitutions of all kinds also face a wide range of regulatory and consumer pressures to buy green. For instance, many governments now offer rebates, tax breaks, and other economic incentives to encourage businesses, schools, individuals, and other consumers to invest in everything from energy-efficient appliances to alternatively fueled vehicles.[1] In 2002, the U.S. Archdiocese of Los Angeles received thousands of dollars in local rebates when the Cathedral of Our Lady of the Angels became the city's first religious edifice to install solar panels on its roof, generating enough energy to power both the building and more than 60 additional residences.[2]

Governments are also using their regulatory authority to essentially force institutions to make greener purchases. Many countries have passed new laws or regulations that require manufacturers to meet certain standards for energy efficiency or recyclability, thus influencing the way companies design and make their products. Vehicle manufacturers, for instance, have had to rethink both their sourcing and use of materials in order to meet the terms of a new European Union directive on end-of-life vehicles, which aims to reduce the portion of old cars that ends up in landfills.[3] Under the law, by 2007 85 percent by weight of every new vehicle must be made from recyclable components (currently, vehicle recycling is limited to the 75 percent by weight that is metallic). DaimlerChrysler hopes to exceed this standard and achieve 95 percent recyclability by 2005, in part by boosting its use of recovered plastic and other materials. If widely adopted, this process could save the automobile industry $320 million per year.[4]

---

* The challenge, however, is ensuring that consumers activate the energy-saving features once they have purchased this equipment.

Governments aren't the only ones pushing institutions to buy green. Around the world, individual consumers are beginning to translate personal concerns about their health, the environment, and social justice into greener buying at the household level. Today, some 63 million U.S. adults, or approximately 30 percent of households in the country, engage in some form of environmentally or socially conscious buying, according to a survey by LOHAS Consumer Research.[5] In the United Kingdom, ethical* purchases by individuals—in areas ranging from organic foods to renewable energy—increased 19 percent between 1999 and 2000, six times faster than the overall market in these sectors.[6]

These consumers increasingly expect better environmental performance from the institutions that guide them, the businesses they support, and the products they buy.[7] Manufacturers in the United States report a growing volume of consumer requests for environmental information about their products, such as whether they contain recycled content.[8] The 1999 Millennium Poll on Corporate Social Responsibility found that some 60 percent of consumers in 23 countries now expect companies to tackle key environmental and social issues through their businesses, in addition to making a profit and generating jobs.[9]

Consumer pressure was instrumental in the push to get municipal authorities in Ferrara, Italy, to introduce organic food into local school cafeterias. After a group of concerned parents drew attention to the poor quality of food being served in area kindergartens in 1994, the town established a commission to study the possibility of switching its food procurement. Within four years, Ferrara had systematized the purchasing of organic food into a special procurement request, and by 2000 80 percent of the food served in the city's kindergartens was organic.[10]

Growing numbers of concerned consumers, shareholders, and nongovernmental organizations are also participating in boycotts and other direct actions to pressure companies into

---

* Here, an ethical purchase is defined as a personal purchasing decision that is aligned to human rights, animal welfare, or the environment and that gives consumers a choice between a product and an ethical alternative.

shifting their buying practices—or risk losing customers. In recent years, advocacy groups like the Rainforest Action Network and ForestEthics have organized public actions in the United States and around the world to get leading retailers like Home Depot to stop buying paper and wood products originating in old-growth forests.[11] (See Sidebar 4, pp. 30 and 31.) Michael Marx, executive director of ForestEthics, notes that a key factor behind the success of these campaigns has been their focus on the private sector: "It's important to target corporate customers because they have an image. The goal is to raise the cost of doing business in an environmentally *un*friendly way." Marx believes that boycotts and other public shaming actions can be much more effective tools for pushing environmental change than, for example, lobbying for regulatory action, which could take years or even decades.[12]

In other cases, NGOs are actively partnering with leading corporations to help them redirect their significant purchasing power toward environmental ends. The Alliance for Environmental Innovation, a project of the nonprofit Environmental Defense, is working with companies like Citigroup, Starbucks, Bristol-Myers Squibb, and Federal Express to shift industry purchases of paper, vehicles, and other products.[13] And the new Climate Savers Program, a joint initiative of the Worldwide Fund for Nature and the Virginia-based Center for Energy and Climate Solutions, works with global companies like Johnson & Johnson, IBM, Nike, and Polaroid to boost their energy efficiency and use of green power.[14] Similarly, the World Resources Institute is recruiting leading companies to help meet its goal of developing corporate markets for 1,000 megawatts of new green power by 2010—enough capacity to power 750,000 American homes.[15]

Overcoming Obstacles

For the past few years, economist Julia Schreiner Alves has been trying to push her employer, the state of São Paolo

Pressuring Home Depot To Buy Sustainable Wood Products

In the mid-1990s, the San Francisco-based Rainforest Action Network (RAN) launched a high-profile campaign to pressure Home Depot, the world's largest home improvement retailer, to improve its wood buying practices. The Atlanta-based retailer sells more than $5 billion worth of lumber, doors, plywood, and other wood products annually in its 1,450 stores worldwide.

RAN used consumer boycotts, in-store demonstrations, ad campaigns, and shareholder activism to draw public attention to Home Depot's practice of buying wood products that originate in highly endangered forests in British Columbia, Southeast Asia, and the Amazon. In August 1999, largely in response to this pressure, the company announced that it would phase out all purchases of old-growth wood by the end of 2002. As of January 2003, it had reduced its purchases of Indonesian lauan (a tropical hardwood used in door components) by 70 percent and shifted more than 90 percent of its cedar purchasing to second- and third-generation forests in the United States. Today, the company claims to know the original wood source of roughly 8,900 of its products.

In its policy, Home Depot also pledges to give preference to products certified as coming from sustainably managed forests. (Currently, roughly 1 percent of wood sold worldwide is certified.) Between 1999 and 2002, the number of its suppliers selling wood approved by the Forest Stewardship Council (FSC), a leading forest certification body, jumped from only 5 to 40, and the value of its certified wood purchases soared from $20 million to more than $200 million.

Home Depot's decision had a significant ripple effect on the wider home improvement and home building markets. Within a year of the company's shift in policy, retailers accounting for well over one-fifth of the wood sold for the U.S. home remodeling market, including leading competitors Lowe's and Wickes, Inc., announced that they too would phase out endangered wood products and favor certified wood. Two of the nation's biggest homebuilders also pledged not to buy endangered wood.

These policy shifts have raised the overall standard for the timber industry. With many companies now scrambling to get FSC approval, it could soon be a liability for other wood producers not to get certified. Michael Marx, executive director of ForestEthics, notes that "one statement from Home Depot did more to change British Columbia's logging practices than 10 years of environmental protest."

Sidebar 4 (continued)

But critics worry that Home Depot hasn't gone far enough in using its market power to influence its suppliers. One obstacle has been the higher cost to vendors of buying certified wood or producing synthetic alternatives, though Home Depot has agreed to absorb any price increases. Another challenge has been weaning consumers away from environmentally unsound options. So far, according to the company, few customers are specifically asking for certified wood.

Sources: See Endnote 11 in the Pressures and Drivers section.

in Brazil, to green its government purchasing. Home to 30 million people, São Paolo is second among all Brazilian states in purchasing power. But Alves faces an uphill battle. She is one of the only people in her agency calling for greener purchasing, and says that many of her colleagues, particularly in the purchasing department, are simply insensitive to the potential of green buying to generate positive environmental change.[1]

At a practical level, the success of green purchasing often comes down to the role of the professional purchaser. An institution's procurement department wields considerable power. In the United States, government purchasing departments supervise 50 to 80 percent of total buying.[2] When purchasing is highly centralized, a single decision made by just one or a handful of buyers can have a tremendous ripple effect, influencing the products used by hundreds or even thousands of individuals. As a result, the buying activities of institutional purchasers often have far greater consequences for the planet than the daily choices of most household consumers.

Unfortunately, many purchasers aren't yet harnessing their tremendous power to leverage environmental change. In some cases, they simply aren't aware of the influence they could have. But they also face political, legal, and institutional obstacles at all stages of their work—from establishing a green purchasing program to sealing a green contract or deal. Unless these barriers are addressed and the gap between good intentions and practical results is narrowed, today's pioneering green purchasing initiatives could be swallowed up in the rising swell of consumption.

Because many organizations have no history of environmental responsibility, getting employees to recognize the benefits of adopting more environmentally sound practices can take
time. Purchasers, managers, and product end-users are often
accustomed to the status quo and resistant to new methods that
may complicate their work. Moreover, skepticism about the
functionality of many green products persists. For instance,
many purchasers still avoid buying recycled paper because
they believe it to be of substandard quality, even though these
types of performance problems have largely been overcome.

Selecting a focus for green purchasing can also be a challenge. Should an institution target smaller, off-the-shelf com-
modities like cleaning products, office furniture, and paper, or
bigger-ticket items like buildings and transport? Ideally, the initiative would focus on changes that make the greatest difference overall, in terms of environment benefits and market
influence. But this usually isn't the case.[3] Stuttgart, Germany,
for instance, focuses its green buying primarily on paper,
cleaning products, and computer equipment, even though
80 percent of municipal spending goes for electricity, heating,
and the construction and renovation of buildings.[4]

Ultimately, the target may depend on an institution's environmental priorities, financial and legal constraints, and the
overall ease or likelihood of adopting the changes. The city of
Santa Monica, California, kicked off its green purchasing effort
in 1994 with less-toxic cleaning products because a large body
of knowledge about product alternatives already existed. Without doing too much additional research, buyers were able to
replace traditional cleaners with less-toxic options in 15 of 17
product categories, saving 5 percent on annual costs and
avoiding the purchase of 1.5 tons of hazardous materials per
year.[5]* Japan's Green Purchasing Network, which encourages
consumers of all kinds to buy green, is thought to be particularly successful because it focuses mainly on office supplies and

---

* Santa Monica has since found replacements in all 17 categories, per Dean
Kubani, sustainable program coordinator, Santa Monica, CA, discussion with
Clayton Adams, Worldwatch Institute, 11 April 2003.

electronics. (Some of the group's members, which include local governments, corporations, and nongovernmental organizations, have achieved 100 percent green procurement of these items.[6])

One important way to institutionalize green purchasing is by establishing an explicit written policy or law that reinforces the activity. Copenhagen's strategy, which went into effect in 1998, specified that within two years all office supplies had to be PVC-free, all photocopiers had to use 100 percent recycled paper, all printers had to use double-sided printing, and all toner cartridges had to be reused.[7]

But having a policy on the books doesn't always guarantee that the activity will take place. The United Kingdom's forward-thinking timber procurement rule is a case in point. In 2000, in response to rising worldwide concern about illegal logging, the central government adopted a policy requiring all departments and agencies to "actively seek" to buy wood products certified as coming from sustainably managed forests.[8] A Greenpeace investigation in April 2002, however, revealed that authorities were clearly flouting this law when they refurbished the Cabinet Office in London with endangered sapele timber from Africa.[9] Following up on the incident, the House of Commons Environmental Audit Committee confirmed that there has been "no systematic or even anecdotal evidence of any significant change in the pattern of timber procurement."[10]

Many U.S. green buying laws, too, have failed to live up to expectations. Under the 1976 Resource Conservation and Recovery Act and subsequent updates, federal agencies are required to consider the use of certain recycled, biobased,* and other environmentally preferable products in their procurement and contracting above a specified dollar limit.[11] But two recent reports, by the U.S. Environmental Protection Agency and the U.S. General Accounting Office, found that not only were few federal agencies meeting the green requirements, but the majority of agency purchasers weren't even aware of the rules.[12]

So what's stopping institutions from buying green? Julian

---

* Biobased products are those fuels, chemicals, building materials, and electric power or heat that are produced from biomass.

Keniry, director of the U.S. National Wildlife Federation's Campus Ecology program, says that many green purchasing efforts fall short because organizations don't set strict targets for the activity and there's no system of accountability. "Policies alone aren't enough," she says. "They need to be coupled with the goal-setting process. Otherwise, they're just words on paper." The more specific and quantifiable an institution's goals, the greater the likelihood that green buying will actually happen.[13]

In some cases, institutions don't impose any sanctions for noncompliance, giving purchasers little incentive to abide by the rules. The 2000 EPA survey, for instance, attributed lax federal compliance with U.S. "buy-recycled" laws to weak enforcement; even if purchasers were aware of the rules, they didn't always perceive them to be mandatory. To encourage compliance, Vorarlberg, Austria, now holds a regional contest to reward the most environmentally friendly town hall for its buying practices, while the U.S. state of Massachusetts gives prizes to the most successful state, municipal, and business green purchasers.[14]

At the same time, most institutional accounting systems aren't set up to track purchases of recycled or green products, making it difficult to monitor activity.[15] The ongoing decentralization of many government, university, and other institutional purchasing operations compounds the accountability problem.[16] Canada's large government agencies now issue some 35,000 individual credit cards, allowing employees to select and charge their own supplies up to a fixed dollar limit, while more than half of U.S. federal purchases are charged on government bankcards.[17]

Some institutions are tackling the monitoring problem the old-fashioned way: tallying green purchasing receipts by hand. But others are developing more sophisticated systems. Kolding, Denmark, is creating an electronic form for recording green purchases, while the U.S. government has made headway in getting an automated tracking system for green products into the federal procurement system.[18] Other institutions are avoiding the responsibility altogether, putting the onus on their suppliers. U.S. renewable energy retailer Green

Mountain Energy, for example, requires its paper supplier, Boise Cascade, to provide summary reports on all Green Mountain purchases of recycled paper.[19]

Greening Contracts

I nstitutions also face obstacles when trying to build environmental demands into the actual purchasing process. Most organizations that make high-value purchases engage in some form of competitive bidding,* meaning that they open up their procurement to many potential suppliers when awarding contracts.

Some of the biggest hurdles arise during the product specification phase, when purchasers outline for suppliers the desired attributes of the items they want to buy. In addition to specifying basic requirements for quantity, price, function, or safety, a purchaser would ideally also be able to make environmental demands, such as asking that products are energy efficient or have recycled content—or that the suppliers themselves have green credentials.[1] (See Sidebar 5, p. 36.) Purchasers could also stipulate certain criteria for social justice, though this isn't very common. The government of Belgium, for instance, is considering barring public contracts with companies whose production conditions disrespect human rights or support anti-democratic regimes.[2]

Unfortunately, inserting green demands into the purchasing process is often easier said than done. Because procurement rules often vary depending on the volume, value, or type of purchase, determining whether environmental considerations are compatible with existing procedures can be a challenge. In parts of the developing world, ongoing corruption and weak enforcement in procurement offer buyers little incentive to make the most efficient purchases, much less

* With some purchases, competitive bidding is not possible because only one supplier is technically qualified to do the job, as is the case with many aerospace and defense contracts.

Inserting Environmental Demands Into Contracts

In greening their contracts with suppliers, purchasers can ask that:

• Products display one or more positive environmental attributes, such as recycled content, energy or water efficiency, low toxicity, or biodegradability.

• Products generate less waste, including by containing less packaging or being durable, reusable, or remanufactured. Santa Monica, California, asks its vendors to supply cleaning products in concentrated form to save packaging.

• Products meet certain environmental criteria during manufacturing or production, such as that paper be processed chlorine free or be made out of timber from a sustainably managed forest.

• Suppliers reclaim or take back items such as batteries, electronics equipment, or carpeting at the end of their useful lives. Some U.S. federal agencies now use "closed loop" contracts requiring contractors to pick up used oil products, tires, and toner cartridges for disposal.

• Suppliers themselves have environmental credentials. Some government purchasers in Switzerland give preference to companies that have or are putting in place environmental management systems.

Sources: See Endnote 1 for this section.

buy environmentally preferable products.[3] Environmental or product standards are often so weak that buyers make poor quality, even dangerous, purchases.[4] In South Asia, negotiators of public works contracts are known to disregard quality and environmental concerns and simply go with the lowest bidder, resulting in wasteful and substandard construction of buildings and roads.[5]

As governments worldwide update their procurement procedures and close loopholes that allow for inefficiency, waste, and corruption, this could either lead to more restrictive regulations that make it harder to buy green, or offer new opportunities. The European Commission is now exploring the legal possibilities for green purchasing under the European Union Procurement Directives, which have historically made no reference to environmental concerns. A July 2001 communication examined how green criteria might be integrated into different stages of EU procurement, from product specification to supplier selection.[6]

In addition to ongoing legal uncertainties, green purchasing faces formidable political challenges. As markets for environmentally preferable products grow, industries that have an ongoing stake in conventional production (such as oil companies, fertilizer companies, and other manufacturers of less environmentally sound products), will likely lose out. These interests are using their significant influence over institutional purchasing decisions to prevent product alternatives from gaining ground. For years, Tom Ferguson of Perdue AgriRecycle has attended trade shows and garnered support from government buyers for his organic fertilizer product, which is derived from recycled poultry litter. But he's not breaking into the market, he says, because the federal specification codes don't allow purchasers to buy alternatives like the one he sells. He notes that powerful industry groups, such as the Fertilizer Institute, will protect chemical agribusiness contracts at all costs. And "if the product or service is not in the government spec, then the hands of the government procurer—no matter how well meaning he is—are tied."[7]*

Even when the political climate is more receptive, purchasers face other obstacles to buying green. In most institutions, rules require them to buy the product or service that best meets their needs at the lowest price, which can rule out more expensive environmentally preferable products. Luz Aída Martínez Meléndez, an employee with Mexico's Ministry of Environment and Natural Resources, complains that finding affordable product alternatives is one of the biggest barriers to green purchasing in her agency.[8]

But some institutions are finding innovative ways to address price concerns. In 2001, the city of Chicago and 48 suburbs pooled their jurisdictional resources to buy a larger block

---

* As of April 2003, some progress had been made in efforts to get specifications for biobased fertilizer products into the U.S. Department of Agriculture farm bill.

of electricity at a reduced rate, and will use the savings to meet at least 20 percent of group power needs with renewable sources by 2006.[9] Kansas City and Jackson County in Missouri have agreed to pay a premium of 15 percent more for alternative fuels, cleaning products, and other products they consider environmentally preferable.[10] Other institutions allow purchasers to compare products based on the lifetime cost of ownership, rather than simply the purchase cost—which often reveals the green choice to be cheaper.[11]

Some institutions are passing the extra costs on to product users. In 2001, more than three-quarters of students at Connecticut College agreed to a voluntary $25 increase in their activity fees to fund the school's transition to renewable energy.[12] By January 2003, the school was supplying 22 percent of its annual electricity consumption from new wind energy, the largest share purchased by any U.S. college or university.[13]

Another serious obstacle to green purchasing is knowing exactly what to look for. Relatively little is known about the environmental characteristics of most products and services on the market today, making it tough for purchasers to compare products effectively.[14] Tracing a product's origins up the chain of production can be particularly challenging. A purchaser may unwittingly buy paper originating from virgin forests in Southeast Asia (where forests are rapidly being cleared for agriculture and other purposes) because it has been repackaged and sold under so many different brand names that even most vendors can't confirm where it comes from.[15] Without the time or scientific background to extensively research green product offerings, many purchasers simply prefer to be told what to buy.[16]

The absence of sound environmental information has led to ongoing confusion among manufacturers, environmentalists, and others about what exactly constitutes a "green" product or service.[17] (Should an "environmentally sound" paper contain a maximum percentage of recycled content? Come from a sustainably harvested forest? Be processed chlorine free? Or some combination of the above? [18]) For many green products, widely recognized environmental standards or specifications don't yet exist.[19] In some cases, green products are so innovative that only a handful of companies produce them, or they undergo such a high rate of technological change that standards or specifications simply haven't been developed.[20] Yet without agreement on what's really "green," manufacturers may remain reluctant to invest in more environmentally sound technologies.

Fortunately, sophisticated tools are being developed to help both manufacturers and purchasers more easily evaluate the environmental performance of products. One particularly promising technique, life-cycle assessment (LCA), offers a methodology for identifying and quantifying the inputs, outputs, and potential environmental impacts of a given product or service throughout its life.[21] (See Figure 3, page 40.) Volvo, for instance, now uses life-cycle considerations to provide detailed information on the various environmental impacts that arise during vehicle manufacturing and use.[22] And the U.S. Department of Commerce's new BEES software (Building for Environmental and Economic Sustainability) uses life-cycle data to help buyers compare and rate the environmental and economic performance of building materials based on their relative impacts in areas like global warming, indoor air quality, resource depletion, and solid waste.[23]

Agreement is also emerging, at least among some stakeholders, on how to define certain green goods, such as paper and cleaning products. In November 2002, a group of 56 environmental groups across North America adopted a set of common environmental criteria for environmentally preferable paper and released detailed guidance to advise paper buyers about their choices.[24] That same year, government purchasers, industry representatives, and environmental groups joined forces under a new North American Green Purchasing Initiative to develop uniform criteria and contract language for green purchases of energy, paper, and cleaning products. One working group scored a big victory by agreeing on a single set of criteria for identifying green cleaning products in government contracts (previously, purchasers had used up to 17 different types of contract language).[25]

Many purchasers (and other consumers) also seek guid-

FIGURE 3

Product Life-Cycle

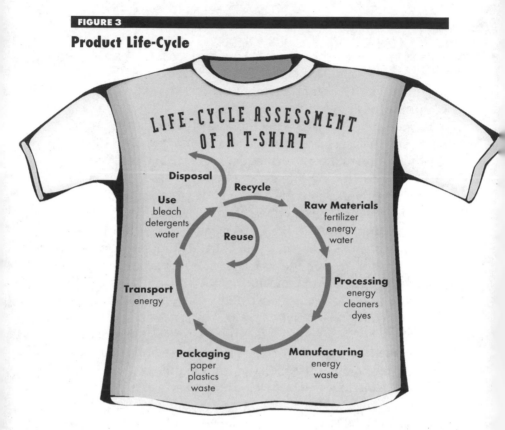

LIFE-CYCLE ASSESSMENT OF A T-SHIRT

Disposal

Recycle

Use
bleach
detergents
water

Reuse

Raw Materials
fertilizer
energy
water

Transport
energy

Processing
energy
cleaners
dyes

Packaging
paper
plastics
waste

Manufacturing
energy
waste

ance from national, regional, and global ecolabeling initiatives. Ecolabels are seals of approval used to indicate that a product has met specified criteria for environmental soundness during one or more stages of its life cycle. Though the range of products and services that carry ecolabels is relatively small, labels can now be found on everything from green electricity services to wood products.[26] (See Sidebar 6.) Certifiers include government agencies, nongovernmental groups, professional or private groups, and international accreditation bodies.

Some institutions allow their purchasers to specifically call for ecolabeled items in their contracts. The city of Ferrara, Italy, for instance, seeks to buy paper that carries the Nordic Swan ecolabel.[27] But many purchasers (particularly government purchasers) hesitate to endorse specific ecolabeled products, ask-

Selected Ecolabeling and Certification Schemes

Product	Certifying Body	Description
Forest products	Forest Stewardship Council	Grants its logo to products obtained from forestry operations that meet specified standards for sustainable management and harvesting. Has certified more than 31 million hectares of forests in 56 countries.
Food products	Rainforest Alliance Conservation Agriculture Network	Awards its logo to coffee, banana, cocoa, and citrus farms that adhere to specified environmental and social standards. As of December 2002, had certified 65,009 hectares in 474 farms and cooperatives in 12 countries, mainly in Central America.
Seafood	Marine Stewardship Council	Has certified seven fisheries (rock lobster, cockles, hoki, mackerel, herring, salmon, and nephrops) that meet set standards for environmentally sound management. Some 126 MSC-labeled products are now sold in 30 outlets in 10 countries.
Energy	Green-e Certification	Rewards retail electricity services in the United States that obtain at least half of their supply from renewable sources. Has certified 27 renewable energy products offered by 16 different suppliers.
Buildings	U.S. Green Building Council's LEED*program	Awards its platinum, gold, silver, and LEED ratings to buildings that have met certain environmental standards for construction and renovation, operations, and commercial interiors.
Electronics	Sweden's TCO '95 label	Identifies computer equipment that has met tough standards for energy consumption, recycling, and reduced toxicity.

*Leadership in Energy and Environmental Design.
Sources: See Endnote 26 for this section.

ing instead that their suppliers satisfy the labels' underlying criteria. The state of Pennsylvania has stated a desire to buy only cleaning products and paints that meet criteria set by Green Seal, a U.S. nonprofit organization that has developed rigorous environmental standards in some 30 product categories.[28] A leading concern is that singling out specific labeled products could create an unfair barrier to trade under the rules of the

World Trade Organization, by discriminating against smaller suppliers that may not be able to meet the costs of qualifying for and complying with the labels.[29] (See Sidebar 7.)

There has been significant industry opposition to ecolabeling, particularly in the United States. Green Seal president Arthur Weissman explains that manufacturers like Proctor & Gamble, a leading producer of household goods, have used a variety of tactics, from legal arguments to extensive government lobbying, to prevent green certified products from entering the U.S. marketplace.[30] "The way they see it, it interrupts the relationship to the consumer," says Weissman. "A third party interferes with the brand."[31]

In some cases, global manufacturers with multiple product lines have resisted efforts to single out any of their products as environmentally preferable out of a concern that this might make their more conventional offerings look bad. "Once companies begin identifying some of their products as environmentally preferable, customers will want to know what's wrong with the other products," explains Scot Case, director of procurement strategies for the Center for a New American Dream. "A company could face legal liabilities if customers suddenly learn that many of its cleaning products, for example, are a toxic witches' brew of known carcinogens and reproductive toxins."[32]

Besides ecolabeling, a variety of other tools also now helps purchasers more easily identify environmentally preferable products and services. Many organizations now publish green purchasing guidelines or product lists for their purchasers to reference, or provide detailed training manuals to lead purchasers through the buying process. The U.S. EPA, for example, offers recommendations for purchasing some 54 different recycled-content products, including traffic cones, toner cartridges, plastic lumber, garden hoses, and building insulation.[33] The city of Göteborg, Sweden, holds training seminars, lectures, and workshops to inform purchasers and other stakeholders about legal requirements, specific tools, and best practices for green procurement. By 2000, 80 to 90 percent of municipal staff (both purchasers and end users) had been trained on green purchasing.[34]

Green Purchasing and the WTO

Some 30 countries have signed (and many more have adopted) the World Trade Organization's Agreement on Government Procurement, which aims to facilitate trade by making it easier for foreign suppliers and their products to access domestic procurement markets. Negotiated in 1979 and updated several times since then, the agreement applies to all public purchases of goods, services, and public works above a certain threshold value, set by each treaty member (usually around $200,000).

Because the WTO agreement makes no explicit reference to the environment, its compatibility with green purchasing remains unclear. The rules generally allow government purchasers to include environmental performance criteria in their product specifications and to set these requirements as high as they desire. (Purchasers must refer to an international standard if it exists.) But there is concern that green purchasing could discriminate against smaller suppliers, particularly in developing countries, that might not be able to meet the higher standards or production costs associated with providing green products.

For example, specifications that favor ecolabeled products (such as FSC-certified timber) could be perceived as discriminatory against producers that may not be able to afford the higher costs of qualifying for and complying with the labels. Similarly, a preference for recycled paper, reflecting a domestic response to high landfill costs, could be perceived as discriminatory against foreign companies that sell paper with high virgin content. And a demand for locally produced food (which releases fewer pollutants in transport) could be perceived as discriminatory against foreign items, which are usually shipped greater distances.

So far, no conflicts between green purchasing and the WTO rules have been registered. But a near precedent occurred in 1996 when the U.S. state of Massachusetts decided to ban from its contracts all companies that had ongoing economic relations with Burma, a country with a poor human rights record. The European Union and Japan registered a complaint with the WTO, arguing that this could represent an unfair barrier to trade. A U.S. court declared the state's action illegal before the case reached the WTO, so a ruling was never issued. Nevertheless, the case illustrates the potential for future conflict between WTO rules and certain purchasing demands.

Sources: See Endnote 29 for this section.

Spreading the Movement

For many years, the effort to publicize and promote greener purchasing practices was scattershot, with much duplication of effort and little cross-fertilization of ideas. But this is beginning to change. Today, initiatives at the international, regional, and local levels seek to both address the obstacles to green purchasing and to accelerate its adoption. And as more institutions recognize the benefits, they are beginning to share information and to learn from each other's successes and failures.

A number of organizations and networks, mainly in Europe, North America, and Japan, now publish green purchasing information, collect success stories, and publicize trends. (See Appendix, page 51, for a list of key groups.) They primarily target institutions with significant purchasing power, such as governments and large corporations, though many of their strategies are also applicable at a smaller scale. Some of these groups partner directly with industry leaders and government officials to encourage greener purchasing. Others rally the grassroots to boycott or otherwise pressure manufacturers or other institutions to change their buying practices. Many also use their resources to promote public debate and generate media interest in the green purchasing movement.

ICLEI's Eco-Procurement Program, launched in 1996, is a leader in promoting green purchasing among governments, businesses, and other institutions across Europe. More than 50 cities and other local governments in 20 countries now belong to the group's Buy-It-Green Network, which helps members exchange information and experiences, join forces, and make joint green purchases.[1] The organization also holds yearly conferences and publishes a magazine that is distributed to more than 5,000 purchasers in Europe. And in one of the first efforts of its kind, ICLEI is working on a project to quantify the environmental savings associated with green purchasing, in order to determine how best to strategically join the purchasing power of cities and to spread green purchasing across Europe.[2] For instance, the project has found that replacing the 2.8 million desktop computers that EU governments buy annually with energy efficient models could reduce European emissions by more than 830,000 tons of carbon dioxide equivalent.[3]

In North America, a leading proponent of institutional green purchasing is the U.S. EPA's Environmentally Preferable Purchasing program, created in 1993 by presidential executive order.[4] The program offers support and information in such areas as construction, office products, conferencing and printing services, cleaning products, cafeteria procurement, and electronics. EPA has also launched several pilot projects, including partnerships with the Department of Defense (to green military operations and installations) and with the National Park Service (to help parks both green their purchasing and educate visitors about their own consumption). The EPA also serves as a clearinghouse through its central database of information on more than 600 environmentally preferable products and services, including links to 130 local, state, and federal green contract specifications; 523 product environmental performance standards; and 25 lists of vendors and products that meet these standards.[5]

The Maryland-based Center for a New American Dream helps large purchasers, particularly state and local governments, incorporate environmental considerations into their purchasing decisions.[6] The Center's Procurement Strategies Program was an active driver behind the new North American Green Purchasing Initiative in 2002, which aims to generate a critical mass for green purchasing on the continent.[7] The group also hopes to serve as a central clearinghouse for green purchasing information for manufacturers, purchasers, and suppliers. It hosts training seminars and nationwide conference calls to teach institutional purchasers how to identify and buy environmentally preferable products, and recently released a video introducing environmental purchasing and describing key success stories.[8]

Japan's Green Purchasing Network (GPN) now boasts some 2,730 member organizations, including more than 2,100 businesses (among them Panasonic, Sony, Fuji, Xerox, Toyota, Honda, Canon, Nissan, and Mitsubishi); 360 local authorities in places like Tokyo, Osaka, Yokohama, Kobe, Sapporo, and Kyoto; and 270 consumer groups, co-ops, and other non-governmental groups.[9] GPN holds countrywide seminars and exhibitions on green purchasing, publishes purchasing guidelines and environmental data books on different products and services, and offers awards to exemplary organizations.

In higher education, more than 275 university presidents and chancellors in over 40 countries have signed on to the 1990 Talloires Declaration, a 10-point action plan that, among other things, encourages universities to establish policies and practices of resource conservation, recycling, waste reduction, and environmentally sound operations.[10] In the hospitality industry, the International Hotels Environment Initiative, a global nonprofit network of more than 8,000 hotels in 11 countries, sponsors a web-based tool to help hotels improve their environmental performance (and save money) through purchases of items from energy-efficient lighting to environmentally preferable flooring materials, refrigerators, and minibars.[11]

There are also efforts to direct greater media attention to green purchasing. In February 2001, the Danish Environmental Protection Agency launched an intensive television, newspaper, and leaflet campaign to raise interest in products carrying ecolabels.[12] Japan's Green Purchasing Network has worked hard to feature green purchasing prominently on television, in newspapers, and at government or corporate seminars.[13] Organizations of all kinds also now use the Internet to inform their buyers about green purchasing, offering procedural tips and links to alternative products and services. King County, in the U.S. state of Washington, uses its comprehensive website and e-mail bulletins to disseminate success stories and other green purchasing developments.[14]

There are also fledgling efforts to spread green purchasing more widely in the developing world, though considerable work remains to be done. ICLEI's new ERNIE* program, supported by the Global Environment Facility, is working with local authorities in several cities—including São Paulo, Brazil; Dur-

* Eco-Responsible Purchasing in Developing Countries and Nearly Industrialized Economies.

ban, South Africa; and Puerto Princessa, Philippines—to develop green purchasing pilot projects.[15] The initiative focuses mainly on buying energy-efficient appliances, and aims to address the various market and other barriers to green procurement, including the areas of transparency, vendor non-discrimination, and capacity-building for local suppliers and manufacturers.

One way institutions can help spread green purchasing to the developing world is by using their own procurements to strengthen local green markets. For instance, the United Nations, World Bank, donor agencies, and multinational corporations that operate in these countries can seek to buy a greater portion of their goods and services from local green suppliers, helping to build capacity for sustainable production.[16] Since 1992, DaimlerChrysler has tapped Brazil's rainforests for environmentally sound coconut fiber and natural rubber, which it now uses in car seats, armrests, and headrests.[17] In doing so, the automaker has not only eliminated the use of synthetic inputs in these vehicle parts, but has also boosted local markets for renewable materials and generated income and employment for farmers.

In most cases, however, it's a big enough challenge simply to get international institutions to buy from developing countries, much less buy green. While some of these institutions do try to buy locally, their procurement generally favors businesses in the industrial world. (Some donor agencies tie their aid to purchases back home.) In 2000, only about a third of the procurements by the UN system went to the developing world.[18] Occasionally, these institutions make socially responsible demands in their purchasing: UNICEF, for instance, seeks to develop sourcing policies and strategies that support national goals for boosting children's welfare.[19] But so far, they have rarely specified environmental criteria, in part because there is a risk that putting green specifications in contracts could alienate smaller suppliers that may not be able to meet these criteria.[20]

By boosting green purchases in developing countries, international institutions can not only stimulate markets but also clean up their own acts in the face of mounting criticism about the environmental impacts of their activities. There is rising interest, for instance, in inserting environmental criteria into the procurements associated with World Bank lending, as part of larger efforts to green the Bank's operations.[21] (See Sidebar 8.)

In 2001, a coalition of multilateral development banks, the United Nations Environment Programme, nongovernmental organizations, and other leading global institutions interested in promoting green purchasing formed an Inter-Agency Sustainable Procurement Group to stimulate such activity both within and outside member institutions.[22] The group hopes to also mainstream the idea of incorporating social criteria into procurement decisions (for example, not buying clothing produced using child labor or under substandard conditions, or purchasing fairly traded goods).

Clearly, the world's institutions have significant power to bring about environmental and social change through their purchases. But green purchasing will never be a magic solution to the world's consumption problems. No matter how environmentally sound this purchasing is, it still involves the use of resources and generation of wastes. Truly reversing global consumption patterns will require not just shifts in buying behavior, but a fundamental rethinking of our wants and needs.

Ultimately, green purchasing shouldn't simply be about buying environmentally preferable products. It should also be about consuming less in general. Institutions should find ways to meet their needs without buying new products—for instance, by eliminating unnecessary purchases and extending the lives of products already in use. Pori, Finland, has implemented a citywide service for reusing goods that enables employees from any municipal department to trade or give away products they no longer need or use.[23] And since 1994, the University of Wisconsin-Madison's SWAP (Surplus With a Purpose) project (which has since been expanded statewide) has helped to divert reusable office furniture, computers, and other goods away from landfills and to other users on campus and around the state.[24]

Nevertheless, green purchasing is an important step on

SIDEBAR 8

Greening Procurement at the World Bank

In 2001, president James Wolfensohn pledged greater support for green purchasing as part of a larger push to "transform the Bank into a global leader on social and environmental responsibility." Two years later, the Bank launched a new Environmentally and Socially Responsible Procurement (ESRP) initiative to further institutionalize its green purchasing.

So far, efforts have focused mainly on internal operations. Each year, the World Bank spends some $500 million on everything from computer equipment to construction contracts to meet the needs of its 10,000 employees in 100 offices worldwide. One of its earliest forays into green purchasing involved buying shade grown coffee for cafeterias. And starting in the late 1990s, the Bank began to consider its wider energy footprint, auditing its offices and examining the carbon emissions associated with appliances, vehicles, and travel.

Now, under the new ESRP policy, purchasers must expand their use of environmentally preferred products. Achievements to date include purchases of 10 percent of energy from renewable sources, paper that is elemental chlorine free and originates from sustainably managed forests, Energy Star-certified copiers, printer toner cartridges with 100 percent soy-based inks, and 100 percent recycled napkins for cafeterias. The Bank has also begun a transition to compact fluorescent lamps.

Yet these changes are small compared to the more daunting challenge of greening external procurement. Each year, the Bank lends some $25 billion to more than 100 countries, which use these funds to buy goods and services for development-related projects. In total, it awards some 40,000 contracts annually to private firms for project assistance.

Traditionally, environmental impact assessments for World Bank projects have considered only the effects of infrastructure placement, not of the materials or equipment used. But the Bank is now examining ways to insert environmental criteria into the technical specifications for project purchasing. (This means, for example, changing language that requires all goods to be new and unused and allowing for purchases of recycled or reconditioned goods.) Initially, it hopes to explore the use of greener pest management criteria in Bank-supported agricultural projects and the adoption of international labor standards in construction contracts. An important model is the Asian Development Bank (ADB), which is a leader among development banks in efforts to convince member countries to align their policies and procedures with ADB environmental requirements.

Sidebar 8 (continued)

World Bank purchasers use an exclusion list for internal procurement that discourages or bans purchases of certain "undesirable" products, such as tobacco and arms. But this hasn't yet been widely applied to environmentally unsound purchases—or to Bank investments or lending.

However, "it is inevitable that we're going in that particular direction," says World Bank lawyer Charles di Leva. The idea is to expand the list to also include substances that cause unnecessary and avoidable environmental damage, such as toxic cleaning agents, asbestos-containing products, and certain pesticides.

In 2002, the World Bank for the first time hired a staff person to focus specifically on green purchasing issues, and headquarters procurement staff underwent environmental training. As it moves ahead with its green purchasing efforts, the Bank plans to share these experiences with other multilateral development banks and international institutions worldwide.

Sources: See Endnote 21 for this section.

the way to achieving a more sustainable world. By raising social consciousness about the environmental impacts of our buying practices, and by motivating governments, businesses, and other institutions to introduce environmental considerations into their decision-making, we can begin to transform the economy.

Appendix

Selected Green Purchasing Resources

The chances of getting a successful green procurement program going can be enhanced by adhering to certain principles, such as winning high-level support, establishing clear policies and goals, offering incentives and monitoring activity, implementing pilot projects, engaging and training stakeholders, highlighting green products, and developing joint purchasing programs. The organizations listed below can serve as invaluable sources of guidance, training, and/or support for these efforts.

General Information

Center for a New American Dream's Procurement Strategies Program
  (www.newdream.org/procure)
Helps U.S. state and local governments and other large purchasers incorporate environmental considerations into their purchasing. Publishes success stories of pioneering efforts and conducts training sessions and conference calls to teach purchasers how to identify and buy greener products.

Consumer's Choice Council
  (www.consumerscouncil.org)
An association of 66 environmental, consumer, and human rights groups from 25 countries that supports ecolabeling and seeks to ensure that consumers have the information they need to purchase greener, more socially just products.

Environmentally Preferable Purchasing Program and Database,
  U.S. Environmental Protection Agency
  (www.epa.gov/oppt/epp)
Comprehensive source of information on green purchasing. Database includes green contract language and specifications, voluntary standards and guidelines, and other practical information.

European Green Purchasing Network
  (www.epe.be/programmes/egpn)
A network that aims to bring together governments, businesses, and other purchasers to promote sustainable innovation and competitiveness along the entire supply chain.

European Union Coalition for Green and Social Procurement
  (www.eeb.org/activities/product_policy/main.htm)
NGO coalition that aims to strengthen environmental and social provisions in EU procurement policies, including consideration of environmental, health, and labor impacts.

GreenOrder
  (www.greenorder.com)
A New York-based consulting firm that helps Fortune 500 companies and top government agencies green their procurement and operations.

Green Seal
   (www.greenseal.org)
An independent organization that certifies and promotes green products
and services and works with manufacturers, industry, purchasing groups,
and governments to green the production and purchasing chain.

NFORM
   (www.informinc.org)
A research organization that provides information on ways to reduce the
environmental impacts of the U.S. economy through improved product
design and greener purchasing.

International Council for Local Environmental Initiatives,
   Eco-Procurement Programme
   (www.iclei.org/europe/ecoprocura/index.htm)
Offers a wide range of information on green purchasing in Europe.
Includes links to the Buy-It-Green Network of municipal purchasers as well
as to success stories, recommendations, and ongoing projects.

IJapan's Green Purchasing Network
   (www.gpn.jp)
An association of some 2,700 organizations, including corporations,
government authorities, and environmental and consumer groups, that
promotes the ideas and practices of green purchasing in Japan.

Massachusetts Environmentally Preferable Products Procurement Program
   (www.state.ma.us/osd/enviro/enviro.htm)
Information about state efforts to buy green products, including useful
guides and reports as well as contracts for purchasing recycled products and
other goods.

National Wildlife Federation Campus Ecology Program
   (www.nwf.org/campusecology/index.cfm)
Provides information to help colleges and universities become living models of an ecologically sustainable society, including by greening their purchasing practices.

North American Commission for Environmental Cooperation, Trade in
   Environmentally Preferable Goods and Services Project
   (www.cec.org/programs_projects/trade_environ_econ)
Aims to build North American markets for renewable energy and other
green products and to facilitate green trade through ecolabeling and green
purchasing. Serves as the Secretariat for the North American Green
Purchasing Initiative, a clearinghouse of information for manufacturers,
purchasers, and suppliers.

Organisation for Economic Co-operation and Development
   (www.oecd.org)
A source of information on coordinating and promoting green public purchasing in industrial countries.

Recycled Products Purchasing Cooperative
  (www.recycledproducts.org/index.html)
A cooperative of U.S. businesses and public institutions that have joined their purchasing power to encourage suppliers to offer recycled paper and other products at reduced rates.

United Nations Environment Programme Sustainable Procurement Website
  (www.uneptie.org/pc/sustain/procurement/green-proc.htm)
Offers information about UN and multilateral efforts to promote sustainable procurement and links to a database listing initiatives worldwide as well as product-specific criteria.

Guidelines, Standards, and Ecolabeling Schemes

Canada's Environmental Choice program
  (www.environmentalchoice.com)
A national ecolabeling program that awards its EcoLogo to products that meet specific guidelines developed through a public consultation process.

EnerGuide
  (energuide.nrcan.gc.ca)
A program run by Natural Resources Canada that provides energy ratings for specific appliance brands as well as additional information on energy efficiency.

Energy Star
  (www.energystar.gov)
A program sponsored by the U.S. Environmental Protection Agency that sets energy-efficiency standards for computers, monitors, printers, and other appliances and certifies green buildings.

European Union Eco-Label
  (europa.eu.int/comm/environment/ecolabel)
A voluntary scheme to help consumers in Europe identify officially approved green products.

Global Ecolabeling Network
  (www.gen.gr.jp)
A nonprofit network of ecolabeling organizations worldwide.

Scientific Certification Systems
  (www.scs1.com)
A neutral, third-party certifier of the food industry and of the environmentally sound management of forests, marine habitats, and manufacturing-related businesses.

Endnotes

Introduction

1. Paul Rauber, "When Uncle Sam Wants Us," *Sierra*, January/February 2003.

2. Jane Holtz Kay, "I Want You...To Buy More Stuff!" *Grist Magazine*, 14 December 2001.

3. United Nations Development Programme, *Human Development Report 1998* (New York: 1998), p. 1.

4. The Progressive Policy Institute, "The New Economy Index: Understanding America's Economic Transformation" (Washington, D.C.: November 1998), www.neweconomyindex.org/section1_page09.html, viewed 13 January 2003.

5. Organisation for Economic Co-operation and Development, cited in United Nations Department of Economic and Social Affairs, Division for Sustainable Development, "Consumer Protection and Sustainable Consumption: New Guidelines for the Global Consumer," background paper for the United Nations Inter-Regional Expert Group Meeting on Consumer Protection and Sustainable Consumption: New Guidelines for the Global Consumer, São Paulo, Brazil, 28–30 January 1998.

6. Alan Durning, *How Much Is Enough?* (New York: W.W. Norton & Co., 1992).

7. Paul Hawken, "The Price of Beauty," *Sierra*, January/February 1998, p. 19.

8. UNDP, op. cit. note 3, p. 2.

9. UNDP, op. cit. note 3, pp. 50, 51.

10. World Resources Institute, United Nations Environment Programme, and World Business Council for Sustainable Development, *Tomorrow's Markets: Global Trends and Their Implications for Business* (Washington, D.C., Paris, and Geneva: 2002), p. 10.

11. Figure 1 data derived by Redefining Progress and cited in Jonathan Loh, ed., *Living Planet Report 2002* (Cambridge, U.K.: World Wide Fund for Nature, June 2002), pp. 21, 22, 26.

12. Michael Scholand, "Compact Fluorescents Set Record," in Worldwatch Institute, *Vital Signs 2002* (New York: W.W. Norton & Co., 2003), pp. 46, 47.

13. Janet Sawin, "Charting a New Energy Future," in Worldwatch Institute, *State of the World 2003* (New York: W.W. Norton & Co., 2003), pp. 85–109.

14. Worldwatch Institute, "Fact Sheet: New Organic Standard To Hit U.S. Shelves on October 21," press release (Washington, D.C.: 9 October 2002); U.S.

Department of Energy, Office of Transportation Technologies, "Hybrid Electric Vehicles in the United States," available at www.ott.doe.gov/facts/archives/fotw230.shtml.

15. Estimates are conservative, per Natural Business Institute, "Understanding the LOHAS Market Report: LOHAS Market Size," www.naturalbusiness.com/market.html, viewed 12 December 2002.

16. GDP data from David Malin Roodman, "Economic Growth Falters," in Worldwatch Institute, *Vital Signs 2002* (New York: W.W. Norton & Co., 2003), pp. 58, 59.

17. Gerard Gleason, associate director, Conservatree, San Francisco, discussion with Clayton Adams, Worldwatch Institute, 7 April 2003.

18. Sawin, op. cit. note 13.

The Power of Procurement

1. Data in Figure 2 are based on 1991 prices and purchasing power parities, per Organisation for Economic Co-operation and Development, *Greener Public Purchasing: Issues and Practical Solutions* (Paris: 2000), p. 36.

2. Commission of the European Communities, *Commission Interpretative Communication on the Community Law Applicable to Public Procurement and the Possibilities for Integrating Environmental Considerations Into Public Procurement* (Brussels: 4 July 2001), p. 5.

3. Estimate of 18 percent is based on a combined continental GDP of $11.7 trillion. Chantal Line Carpentier, North American Commission for Environmental Cooperation, presentation at North American Green Purchasing Conference, Philadelphia, Pennsylvania, 22–24 April 2002.

4. Scot Case, Center for a New American Dream, e-mail to author, 11 April 2003.

5. Adidas-Salomon, *Social and Environmental Report 2002* (Herzogenaurach, Germany: 2003).

6. K. Green, B. Morton, and S. New, *Consumption, Environment, and the Social Sciences,* cited in Adam C. Faruk et al., "Analyzing, Mapping, and Managing Environmental Impacts Along Supply Chains," *Journal of Industrial Ecology,* Spring 2001, p. 15.

7. This figure includes the amount spent by students on books and school supplies. Kevin Lyons, Rutgers University (instructor), "Driving Sustainable Markets 'Teach-In,'" on-line course sponsored by the National Wildlife Federation's Campus Ecology Program and the National Association of Educational Buyers, 2002; 3 percent from U.S. Department of Commerce, Bureau of Economic Analysis, "Current Dollar and 'Real' Dollar Gross Domestic Product," www.bea.doc.gov/bea/dn/gdplev.xls, viewed 7 May 2003; 18 economies from World Bank,

World Development Indicators 2001 (Washington, D.C.: 11 April 2001).

8. Gary Gardner, *Invoking the Spirit: Religion and Spirituality in the Quest for a Sustainable World*, Worldwatch Paper 164 (Washington, D.C.: Worldwatch Institute, December 2002).

9. United Nations Inter-Agency Procurement Services Office, *Annual Statistical Report 2000* (New York: July 2001).

10. Scot Case, op. cit. note 4.

11. Sidebar 1 derived from the following sources: building construction data, computers, CFLs, and beef from Scot Case, Center for a New American Dream, discussion with author, 2 December 2002; carbon dioxide equivalencies from TerraChoice Environmental Services, Inc., *Products and Services: The Climate Change Connection* (Ottawa: March 2002); Peter Bühle et al., *Stuttgart Green Purchasing Status Report* (Freiburg: International Council for Local Environmental Initiatives, January 2002); U.S. Office of the Federal Environmental Executive, "Web Based Paper Calculator," www.ofee.gov/recycled/calculat.htm; Janet N. Abramovitz and Ashley T. Mattoon, *Paper Cuts: Recovering the Paper Landscape*, Worldwatch Paper 149 (Washington, D.C.: Worldwatch Institute, December 1999); 12 million tons from United States Conference of Mayors, Information about the Paper Recycling Challenge, es.epa.gov/techinfo/genrefs/chalenge.html; Alicia Culver et al., *Cleaning for Health: Products and Practices for a Safer Indoor Environment* (New York: INFORM, Inc., 2002).

12. U.S. Office of the Federal Environmental Executive, op. cit. note 11.

13. Environmental Defense, "Catalog Companies Are Selling Nature Short This Holiday Season," press release (New York: 13 November 2002).

14. Janitorial Products Pollution Prevention Project, "What Injuries Happen to Your Janitors?" www.westp2net.org/Janitorial/jp4.htm, viewed 20 February 2003.

15. U.S. Environmental Protection Agency, *Private Sector Pioneers: How Companies Are Incorporating Environmentally Preferable Purchasing* (Washington, D.C.: June 1999); Andrew A. King and Michael J. Lenox, "Does It *Really* Pay to Be Green?" *Journal of Industrial Ecology*, Winter 2001, pp. 105–116.

16. Christoph Erdmenger et al., *The World Buys Green* (Freiburg: International Council for Local Environmental Initiatives, 2001), p. 13.

17. International Council for Local Environmental Initiatives, *Green Purchasing Good Practice Guide* (Freiburg: 2000), p. 21.

18. Will Nixon, "The Color of Money," *The Amicus Journal*, Summer 1998, pp. 16–18.

19. TerraChoice Environmental Services, Inc., op. cit. note 11, p. 20.

20. Alicia Culver et al., op. cit. note 11.

Green Purchasing Pioneers

1. Sidebar 2 based on the following sources: Bank of America, *Environmental Commitment 2001 Activity Highlights*, www.bankofamerica.com/environment/index.cfm, viewed 29 April 2003; Boeing ,"EPA Names Boeing Partner of the Year," press release (St. Louis: 14 April 1999); 16,000 homes from "Sustainability and Green Procurement," *Pollution Prevention Northwest*, Pacific Northwest Pollution Prevention Resource Center, Fall 1999, at www.pprc.org/pprc/pubs/newslets/news1199.html; Canon, *Canon Environmental Report 2002*, www.canon.com/environment/eco2002e/p22.html, viewed 8 April 2003; Federal Express, "FedEx and the Environment," www.fedex.com/us/about/news/ontherecord/environment.html, viewed 29 April 2003; Hewlett-Packard, "Supply Chain Social and Environmental Responsibility," www.hp.com/hpinfo/globalcitizenship/environment/supplychain/index.html, viewed 29 April 2003; IKEA International A/S, *IKEA: Environmental and Social Issues 2001* (Delft, Netherlands: November 2001), p. 13; John Zurcher, IKEA U.S., discussion with Clayton Adams, Worldwatch Institute, 8 April 2003; McDonald's from U.S. Environmental Protection Agency, *Private Sector Pioneers: How Companies Are Incorporating Environmentally Preferable Purchasing* (Washington, D.C.: June 1999), pp. 20–22 and from "McDonald's Approves Earthshell Container for Big Mac," *Environment News Service*, 2 April 2001; William Hall, "Migros Commits To Buying Green Palm Oil," *Financial Times*, 24 January 2002; Patagonia, "Organic Cotton: What We Do," www.patagonia.com/enviro/organic_cotton.shtml, viewed 29 April 2003; Riu Hotels from International Hotels Environment Initiative, "Case Studies," www.ihei.org/HOTELIER/hotelier.nsf/content/c1b2.html, viewed 9 May 2003; Staples, Inc., "How Staples Recycles," www.staples.com/products/centers/recycle/hsr.asp, viewed 16 April 2003; Staples, Inc., "Staples Environmental Paper Procurement Policy" (Framingham, Massachusetts: November 2002), viewed 16 April 2003; Staples, Inc., "Staples Joins Green Power Market Development Group," press release (13 March 2003); Starbucks, "Coffee, Tea, & Paper Sourcing," www.starbucks.com/aboutus/sourcing.asp, viewed 29 April 2003; Toyota, "Procurement/Production/Logistics," www.toyota.co.jp/IRweb/corp_info/eco/pro.html, viewed 14 April 2003; Shelley Billik, Warner Brothers, e-mails to Clayton Adams, Worldwatch Institute, 8 April 2003 and 14 April 2003.

2. Amanda Griscom, "In Good Company," *Grist Magazine*, 31 July 2002.

3. U.S. Environmental Protection Agency, *Private Sector Pioneers: How Companies Are Incorporating Environmentally Preferable Purchasing* (Washington, D.C.: June 1999), p. 22.

4. Craig R. Carter and Marianne M. Jennings, *Purchasing's Contribution to the Socially Responsible Management of the Supply Chain* (Tempe, Arizona: CAPS Research, 2000), p. 11.

5. Steven A. Melnyk et al., *ISO 14000: Assessing Its Impact on Corporate Effectiveness and Efficiency* (Tempe, Arizona: CAPS Research, 1999), p. 20.

6. Heidi McCloskey, Nike Apparel, conversation with Brian Halweil, Worldwatch Institute, 18 February 2003.

7. Nike, Inc., "Team Players," at www.nike.com/nikebiz/nikebiz, viewed 28 February 2003.

8. Ibid.

9. Recycled Paper Coalition, "About Us," at www.papercoalition.org/aboutus.html, viewed 11 March 2003.

10. Jeffrey Hollender, "Changing the Nature of Commerce," in Juliet B. Schor and Betsy Taylor, eds. *Sustainable Planet: Solutions for the Twenty-first Century* (Boston: Beacon Press, 2002), p. 76.

11. See, for example, United Nations, *Agenda 21* (New York: April 1993, p. 33; Organisation for Economic Co-operation and Development Council, "Recommendation of the Council on Improving the Environmental Performance of Government," (Paris: 1996); International Council for Local Environmental Initiatives, "Lyon Declaration: Enhancing the Framework, Enforcing the Action for Greening Government Operations," text adopted at the Eco-Procura® Lyon Conference, Lyon, France, 17–18 October 2000.

12. United Nations, *Report of the World Summit on Sustainable Development* (New York: 2002), p. 21.

13. Organisation for Economic Co-operation and Development, *Greener Public Purchasing: Issues and Practical Solutions* (Paris: 2000), pp. 19, 20.

14. Sidebar 3 based on the following sources (where no country is mentioned, the source contributed information on several countries): Australia from "National Government Waste Reduction and Purchasing Guidelines," available at www.ea.gov.au/industry/sustainable/greening-govt/waste-reduction.html, viewed 19 March 2003, from United Nations Environment Programme and Consumers International, *Tracking Progress: Implementing Sustainable Consumption Policies* (Nairobi: May 2002), p. 36, and from Environment Australia, "Greening of Government," www.ea.gov.au/industry/sustainable/greening-govt/index.html, viewed 19 March 2003; Canada from Natural Resources Canada, *Government of Canada Action Plan 2000 on Climate Change*, www.climatechange.gc.ca/english/whats_new/pdf/gofcdaplan_eng2.pdf, and Department of Justice, *Alternative Fuels Act 1995*, http://laws.justice.gc.ca/en/A-10.7/text.html; Germany from www.beschaffung-info.de; Center for a New American Dream, "Environmental Purchasing Factoids," at www.newdream.org/procure/factoids.html, viewed 3 March 2003; Organisation for Economic Co-operation and Development (OECD), op. cit. note 13, pp. 50–60; International Council for Local Environmental Initiatives (ICLEI), *Green Purchasing Good Practice Guide* (Freiburg: 2000); Christoph Erdmenger et al., *The World Buys Green* (Freiburg: ICLEI, 2001); Christoph Erdmenger, "Sustainable Purchasing—a Concept Emerging From the Local Level," *International Aid & Trade Review*, Conference & Exhibition 2002 Special Edition, June 19–20,

2002, pp. 124, 125; OECD Trade Directorate, *Trade Issues In the Greening of Public Purchasing* (Paris: 16 March 1999), pp. 4, 5, 28; Hiroyuki Sato, "Green Purchasing in Japan: Progress, Current Status, and Future Prospects" (Tokyo: Green Purchasing Network, 2003); Scot Case, "Moving Beyond 'Buy Recycled,'" *ECOS*, Spring 2001, p. 1; U.S. General Accounting Office, *Federal Procurement: Better Guidance and Monitoring Needed To Assess Purchases of Environmentally Friendly Products* (Washington, D.C.: June 2001), p. 4.

15. Christoph Erdmenger, International Council for Local Environmental Initiatives, "Overview and Recent Developments of Sustainable Procurement," presentation at International Aid and Trade 2002 conference on "Trade and Development: Building Capacity for Sustainable Markets," New York, 19–20 June 2002.

16. Ibid.

17. "The Hannover Call of European Municipal Leaders at the Turn of the 21st Century," available at www.iclei.org/ecoprocura/info/Hann_call.pdf, viewed 24 March 2004.

18. Bente Møller Jensen and Anders Schmidt, *Green Purchasing Status Report: Municipality of Kolding* (Freiburg: International Council for Local Environmental Initiatives, February 2002).

19. Mike Liles, Minnesota Office of Environmental Assistance, e-mail to Clayton Adams, Worldwatch Institute, 9 April 2003.

20. Dean Kubani, City of Santa Monica, California, discussion with Clayton Adams, Worldwatch Institute, 11 April 2003.

21. U.S. Environmental Protection Agency, *State and Local Government Pioneers* (Washington, D.C.: November 2000).

22. Public Construction Commission Executive Yuan, "Article 96," *Government Procurement Law*, www.pcc.gov.tw/c2/c2b/c2b_3/2_b_3_10.htm, viewed 9 May 2003.

23. United Nations Environment Programme and Consumers International, op. cit. note 14, p. 26.

24. United Nations Environment Programme (UNEP), "DRAFT Mapping of Major Procurement Initiatives World-wide," document prepared for the Interagency Group on Sustainable Procurement (Paris: 2003); Thailand from Burton Hamner, Hamner and Associates LLC, Seattle, Washington, e-mail to author, 3 February 2003; Mauritius from UNEP and Consumers International, op. cit. note 14, pp. 54, 55.

25. Erdmenger et al., op. cit. note 14, p. 13.

26. White House Task Force on Recycling, *Greening the Government: A Report* *to the President on Federal Leadership and Progress* (Washington, D.C.: 22 April 2000), p. 25.

27. Jim Motavalli and Josh Harkinson, "Buying Green," *E Magazine*, September/October 2002, p. 29.

28. Luke Brander and Xander Olsthoorn, *Three Scenarios for Green Public Procurement* (Amsterdam: Vrije Universiteit Institute for Environmental Studies, December 2002), p. 16.

29. One million from Christoph Erdmenger et al., op. cit. note 14, p. 59; 7 percent from Scot●se, Center for a New American Dream, discussion with author, 2 December 2002.

30. William J. Clinton, *Executive Order 12845: Requiring Agencies to Purchase Energy Efficient Computer Equipment* (Washington, D.C.: 21 April 1993).

31. Maria Vargas, Climate Protection Partnerships Division, U.S. Environmental Protection Agency, discussion with Clayton Adams, Worldwatch Institute, 25 April 2003.

32. Christoph Erdmenger et al., op. cit. note 14, p. 47.

Pressures and Drivers

1. For vehicle incentives, see the Clean Cities International Program website, at www.ccities.doe.gov.

2. "Los Angeles Cathedral To Use Solar Power," *Reuters*, 19 August 2002.

3. European Commission, "Directive 2000/53/EC of the European Parliament and of the Council of 18 September 2000 on End-of-Life Vehicles," *Official Journal of the European Communities*, 21 October 2000.

4. Chrysler Group, "The Chrysler Group Demonstrates Its 'CARE' for the Environment by Turning Garbage Into Car Parts," press release (Auburn Hills, Michigan: 20 March 2002).

5. Data based on a survey of 2,267 households in November 2001, per LOHAS Consumer Research, "Nearly One-Third of Americans Identified as Values-Based, Highly-Principled Consumers, New Research Shows," press release (Broomfield, Colorado: 19 June 2002).

6. Deborah Doane, *Taking Flight: The Rapid Growth of Ethical Consumerism*, report for the Co-operative Bank (London: New Economics Foundation, October 2001), p. 2.

7. See Robin Broad, ed., *Global Backlash: Citizen Initiatives for a Just World Economy* (Lanham: Rowman & Littlefield, 2002).

8. U.S. Environmental Protection Agency, *Private Sector Pioneers: How Companies Are Incorporating Environmentally Preferable Purchasing* (Washington, D.C.: June 1999), p. 7.

9. Environics International, Ltd., *The Millennium Poll on Corporate Social Responsibility: Executive Briefing* (Toronto: September 1999).

10. International Council for Local Environmental Initiatives, *Green Purchasing Good Practice Guide* (Freiburg: 2000), pp. 23, 24.

11. Sidebar 4 derived from the following sources: Home Depot, "The Journey to Sustainable Forestry," information sheet (Atlanta: January 2003); $5 billion, 1,450 stores, 8,900 products, and certification numbers from Dan Morse, "Home Depot Is Expected To Deliver Report on Timber," *Wall Street Journal*, 2 January 2003; 20 percent from "Home Depot Decision Cheered," *Environmental News Network*, 30 August 1999; competitors from Jim Carlton, "Against the Grain: How Home Depot and Activists Joined To Cut Logging Abuse," *Wall Street Journal*, 26 September 2000; Jim Carlton, "Home Builders Centex and Kaufman Agree Not To Buy Endangered Wood," *Wall Street Journal*, 31 March 2000; scrambling for certification from Barrie McKenna, "U.S. Home Builders To Ban Old-Growth Wood," *Globe and Mail*, 31 March 2000; Michael Marx, Forest Ethics, presentation at North American Green Purchasing Conference, Philadelphia, Pennsylvania, 22–24 April 2002; criticism from Rainforest Action Network, "Rainforest Action Network Statement on Home Depot's Wood Purchasing Policy," press release (San Francisco: 2 January 2003); price increases from June Preston, "Home Depot Says It Aims To Save Ancient Forests," *Environmental News Network*, 30 August 1999.

12. Marx, op. cit. note 11.

13. Alliance for Environmental Innovation website, www.environmentaldefense.org/alliance, viewed 12 May 2003.

14. World Wide Fund for Nature, "WWF Climate Change Programme: Business Partners," at www.panda.org/about_wwf/what_we_do/climate_change/what_we_do/business_industry/climate_savers.cfm, viewed 7 March 2003.

15. World Resources Institute, Green Power Market Development Group website, www.thegreenpowergroup.org.

Overcoming Obstacles

1. Julia Alves, Compañia Estatal de Saneamiento Básico y Tecnologia, São Paulo, Brazil, e-mail to author, 7 April 2003.

2. National Pollution Prevention Roundtable, Environmentally Preferable Purchasing Discussion Group, "Environmentally Preferable Purchasing," PowerPoint presentation, available at www.newdream.org/procure/resources.html#ppt.

3. Luke Brander and Xander Olsthoorn, *Three Scenarios for Green Public Pro-*

curement (Amsterdam: Vrije Universiteit Institute for Environmental Studies, December 2002), pp. 11, 12.

4. Peter Bühle et al., *Stuttgart Green Purchasing Status Report* (Freiburg: International Council for Local Environmental Initiatives, January 2002), pp. 45, 46.

5. U.S. Environmental Protection Agency (USEPA), *The City of Santa Monica's Environmental Purchasing: A Case Study* (Washington, D.C.: March 1998), pp. 1,8; 1.5 tons from USEPA, *State and Local Government Pioneers* (Washington, D.C.: November 2000), p. 24.

6. Hiroyuki Sato, Green Purchasing Network, Tokyo, Japan, e-mail to Clayton Adams, Worldwatch Institute, 21 April 2003.

7. International Council for Local Environmental Initiatives, *Green Purchasing Good Practice Guide* (Freiburg: 2000), p. 42.

8. United Kingdom Department of the Environment, Transport and the Regions, "Action To Halt Illegal Timber Imports—Meacher," press release (London: 28 July 2000).

9. Greenpeace U.K., "Greenpeace Catches Blair Trashing Ancient Forests to Furnish the Cabinet Office," press release (London: 10 April 2002).

10. House of Commons Environmental Audit Committee, "Buying Time for Forests: Timber Trade and Public Procurement," *Sixth Report of Session 2001–02* (London: 24 July 2002), p. 4.

11. "Executive Order 13101—Greening the Government Through Waste Prevention, Recycling, and Federal Acquisition," *Federal Register*, 16 September 1998.

12. U.S. Environmental Protection Agency, *Qualitative Measurement of Environmentally Preferable Purchasing (EPP) Among Federal Employees in 2000* (Washington, D.C.: February 2001); U.S. General Accounting Office, *Federal Procurement: Better Guidance and Monitoring Needed To Assess Purchases of Environmentally Friendly Products* (Washington, D.C.: June 2001).

13. Julian Keniry, National Wildlife Federation, discussion with author, 28 March 2002.

14. Vorarlburg from International Council for Local Environmental Initiatives, op. cit. note 7, p. 39; Massachusetts from Marcia Deegler, Operational Services Division, Commonwealth of Massachusetts, e-mail to Clayton Adams, Worldwatch Institute, 10 April 2003.

15. U.S. General Accounting Office, op. cit. note 12.

16. Tapio Pento, "Implementation of Public Green Procurement Programmes," in Trevor Russel, ed., *Greener Purchasing: Opportunities and Innovations* (Sheffield: Greenleaf Publishing, 1998), pp. 23–30; Organisation for Economic Co-operation and Development, *Greener Public Purchasing: Issues and Practical Solutions* (Paris: 2000), pp. 46, 82.

17. Berny Letreille, Environment Canada, discussion with Clayton Adams, Worldwatch Institute, 14 April 2003; Tom Snyder, Argonne National Laboratory, U.S. Department of Energy, discussion with Clayton Adams, Worldwatch Institute, 9 April 2003.

18. Bente Møller Jensen and Anders Schmidt, *Green Purchasing Status Report: Municipality of Kolding* (Freiburg: International Council for Local Environmental Initiatives, February 2002), p. 12; Holly Ellwood, EPP Program, U.S. Environmental Protection Agency, discussion with Clayton Adams, Worldwatch Institute, 9 April 2003.

19. Matthew DeLuca, Green Mountain Energy Company, Burlington, Vermont, discussion with Clayton Adams, Worldwatch Institute, 4 April 2003.

Greening Contracts

1.   Sidebar 5 derived from the following sources: Kevin Lyons, *Buying for the Future: Contract Management and the Environmental Challenge* (London: Pluto Press, 2000); U.S. Environmental Protection Agency, *The City of Santa Monica's Environmental Purchasing: A Case Study* (Washington, D.C.: March 1998), p. 7; White House Task Force on Recycling, *Greening the Government: A Report to the President on Federal Leadership and Progress* (Washington, D.C.: 22 April 2000), p. 25; Switzerland from Organisation for Economic Co-operation and Development, *Greener Government Purchasing* (Paris: 2000), p. 67.

2.   Anne-Françoise Gailly, "Green Procurement and the Belgian Presidency," *Eco-Procura* (International Council for Local Environmental Initiatives), September 2001, p. 9.

3.   Asian Development Bank, *To Serve and To Preserve: Improving Public Administration In a Competitive World* (Manila: 2000), p. 334.

4.   Christoph Erdmenger, "Sustainable Purchasing—a Concept Emerging From the Local Level," *International Aid & Trade Review*, Conference & Exhibition 2002 Special Edition, June 19–20, 2002, p. 124.

5.   Rafik Meghji, M-Konsult, "Building Capacity in the Market," presentation at International Aid and Trade 2002 conference on "Trade and Development: Building Capacity for Sustainable Markets," New York, 19–20 June 2002.

6.   Commission of the European Communities, *Commission Interpretative Communication on the Community Law Applicable to Public Procurement and the Possibilities for Integrating Environmental Considerations Into Public Procurement* (Brussels: 4 July 2001).

7.   Tom Ferguson, Perdue AgriRecycle, LLC, discussion with author, 22 April 2002, and discussion with Clayton Adams, Worldwatch Institute, 2 April 2003.

8. Luz Aída Martínez Meléndez, Programa de Administracion Sustentable, Ministry of Environment and Natural Resources, Mexico, e-mail to Clayton Adams, Worldwatch Institute, 7 April 2003.

9. Office of the Mayor, Chicago, Illinois, "City Selects ComEd To Provide Clean Power, Leads Nation in Building 'Green' Electricity Market," press release (Chicago: 6 July 2001).

10. U.S. Environmental Protection Agency, *State and Local Government Pioneers* (Washington, D.C.: November 2000), p. 13.

11. Scot Case, Center for a New American Dream, discussion with author, 3 December 2002.

12. Connecticut Energy Co-op, "Connecticut College Is 1st College To Buy Green Power From the Co-op," press release (Hartford: 11 May 2001); Jessica Stine, "Demystifying "Green" Purchasing," *NAEB Journal*, Summer 2001, p. 15.

13. Connecticut College, "Connecticut College Sets National 'Green Energy' Record; Purchases Wind Energy Certificates for 22 Percent of Electricity Use," press release (New London: 27 January 2003).

14. Organisation for Economic Co-operation and Development, op. cit. note 1, p. 57.

15. Paul Brown, Steven Morris, and John Aglionby, "Rainforests Hit By Paper Trail to U.K.," *The Guardian*, 26 June 2001.

16. U.S. Environmental Protection Agency, *Qualitative Measurement of Environmentally Preferable Purchasing (EPP) Among Federal Employees in 2000* (Washington, D.C.: February 2001), p. 8.

17. Jacqueline Ottman, *Green Marketing: Opportunity for Innovation* (New York: NTC-McGraw-Hill, 1998).

18. Recycled Paper Coalition, "RPC Listening Study on Environmental Printing and Office Papers," at www.papercoalition.org/survey.html, viewed 11 March 2003.

19. Organisation for Economic Co-operation and Development Trade Directorate, *Trade Issues In the Greening of Public Purchasing* (Paris: 16 March 1999), p. 18.

20. Environment Canada, *Towards Greener Government Procurement* (Hull, Quebec: updated May 2000).

21. Rita Schenck, "Life Cycle Assessment: the Environmental Performance Yardstick," paper prepared for Earthwise Design, Life Cycle Assessment Realities and Solutions for Sustainable Buildings conference, Antioch University, 19 January 2002.

22. U.S. Environmental Protection Agency, *Private Sector Pioneers: How Com-*

panies Are Incorporating Environmentally Preferable Purchasing (Washington, D.C.: June 1999), p. 9.

23. U.S. Department of Commerce, National Institute of Standards and Technology, Office of Applied Economics, "BEES 3.0," at www.bfrl.nist.gov/oae/software/bees.html.

24. Center for a New American Dream et al., "A Common Vision for Transforming the Paper Industry: Striving for Environmental and Social Sustainability," ratified at the Environmental Paper Summit, Sonoma County, California, 20 November 2002, available at www.conservatree.com/paper/choose/commonvision.shtml, viewed 11 March 2003.

25. Office of the Federal Environmental Executive, "Governments Agree on National Criteria for 'Green' Cleaning Products," press release, at www.ofee.gov/gp/greencleancriteria.htm, viewed 4 March 2003.

26. Sidebar 6 based on the following sources: Forest Stewardship Council data as of December 2002, in "Forests Certified by FSC-Accredited Certification Bodies," www.fscoax.org/html/5-3-3.html, viewed 6 January 2003; Rainforest Alliance, "Conservation Agriculture Network," at www.rainforestalliance.org/programs/cap/faq.html, viewed 17 January 2002; 126 products and 30 outlets from Karen Tarica, Marine Stewardship Council, e-mail to author, 6 January 2003; 27 products and 16 suppliers from Carrie Harvilla, Center for Resource Solutions, San Francisco, CA, e-mail to author, 9 January 2003; U.S. Green Building Council, LEED website, at www.usgbc.org/LEED/LEED_main.asp; Swedish Confederation of Professional Employees, "Dell First on the Market," press release (Stockholm: 29 December 1997).

27. Michele Ferrari, "Ferrara, on Its Way Toward Green Procurement," *EcoProcura* (International Council for Local Environmental Initiatives), September 2001, p. 19.

28. U.S. Environmental Protection Agency, op. cit. note 10, p. 17; Arthur Weissman, Green Seal, discussion with Clayton Adams, Worldwatch Institute, 1 April 2003.

29. Sidebar 7 derived from the following sources: World Trade Organization (WTO), "Government Procurement: The Plurilateral Agreement," www.wto.org/english/tratop_e/gproc_e/gp_gpa_e.htm, viewed 22 April 2003; Organisation for Economic Co-operation and Development Trade Directorate, op. cit. note 19; Doaa Abdel Motaai, Trade and Environment Division, WTO, "Overview and Recent Developments of Sustainable Procurement," presentation at International Aid and Trade 2002 conference on "Trade and Development: Building Capacity for Sustainable Markets," New York, 19-20 June 2002; WTO, "United States—Measure Affecting Government Procurement" (Geneva: 9 September 1998).

30. Jim Motavalli and Josh Harkinson, "Buying Green," *E Magazine*, September/October 2002, p. 29.

31. Arthur Weissman, Green Seal, discussion with author, 8 April 2003.

32. Scot Case, Center for a New American Dream, e-mail to author, 11 April 2003.

33. U.S. Environmental Protection Agency, Comprehensive Procurement Guidelines website, www.epa.gov/cpg.

34. International Council for Local Environmental Initiatives, *Green Purchasing Good Practice Guide* (Freiburg: 2000), p. 36.

Spreading the Movement

1. International Council for Local Environmental Initiatives, "BIG-Net: Buy-It-Green Network," www.iclei.org/europe/ecoprocura/network/index.htm, viewed 4 April 2003.

2. International Council for Local Environmental Initiatives, "RELIEF-European Research Project on Green Purchasing," at www.iclei.org/europe/ecoprocura/relief/index.htm, viewed 4 April 2003.

3. International Council for Local Environmental Initiatives, "Eco-Procurement: The Path to a Greener Marketplace" (Freiburg: 2002).

4. U.S. Environmental Protection Agency, Environmentally Preferable Purchasing website, www.epa.gov/opptintr/epp/index.htm; White House, "Executive Order #12873: Federal Acquisition, Recycling and Waste Prevention," press release (Washington, D.C.: 20 October 1993).

5. U.S. Environmental Protection Agency, Environmentally Preferable Purchasing Database, www.epa.gov/oppt/epp/database.htm, viewed 19 February 2003.

6. Center for a New American Dream website, www.newdream.org.

7. U.S. Environmental Protection Agency, "Conference Helps Further Green Purchasing," *EPP Update*, August 2002, pp. 2, 3.

8. Scot Case, Center for a New American Dream, e-mail to author, 11 April 2003.

9. Hiroyuki Sato, "Green Purchasing in Japan: Progress, Current Status, and Future Prospects" (Tokyo: Green Purchasing Network, 2003).

10. University Leaders for a Sustainable Future, "Programs (Talloires Declaration)," at www.ulsf.org/programs_talloires.html, viewed 4 March 2003.

11. International Hotels Environment Initiative website, www.ihei.org; Benchmark Hotel website, www.benchmarkhotel.com.

12. Christoph Erdmenger et al., *The World Buys Green* (Freiburg: International Council for Local Environmental Initiatives, 2001), p. 33.

13. Green Purchasing Network website, eco.goo.ne.jp/gpn/index.html, viewed 9 April 2003.

14. King County Environmental Purchasing website, www.metrokc.gov/procure/green/index.htm.

15. Christoph Erdmenger, "Sustainable Purchasing—A Concept Emerging From the Local Level," *International Aid & Trade Review*, Conference & Exhibition 2002 Special Edition, June 19–20, 2002, pp. 122–124.

16. Robert Goodland, *Ecolabeling: Opportunities for Progress Toward Sustainability* (Washington, D.C.: Consumer's Choice Council, April 2002), pp. 7, 8.

17. Miriam Jordan, "From the Amazon to Your Armrest," *Wall Street Journal*, 1 May 2001; DaimlerChrysler, *Environmental Report 2001* (Stuttgart/Auburn Hills: 30 July 2001).

18. United Nations Inter-Agency Procurement Services Office, *Annual Statistical Report 2000* (New York: July 2001), p. 5.

19. UNICEF, *Supply Division Annual Report 2001* (New York: 2002), p. 5.

20. Goodland, op. cit. note 16, pp. 9, 10.

21. Sidebar 8 derived from the following sources: World Bank, "Putting Social and 'Green' Responsibility on the Corporate Agenda. World Bank Chief Says Corporate Responsibility Is Key to Sustainable Development—and Good Business," press release (Washington, D.C.: 21 June 2001); Dominique Brief, Environmentally and Socially Responsible Procurement Initiative, World Bank, discussion with Clayton Adams, Worldwatch Institute, 8 April 2003; Maureen M. Moore, Environment Program, General Services Department, World Bank, e-mail to Clayton Adams, Worldwatch Institute, 14 April 2003; Chad Dobson, Consumer's Choice Council, Washington, D.C., discussion with author, 6 May 2003; Bernard Ross, "World Bank Structural Adjustment and Investment Loans: Approaches to Environmental Conditionality in Procurement" (Washington, D.C.: May 2000); World Bank, "Greening the Bank," *Environment Matters*, July 2000–June 2001, p. 55; Charles di Leva, World Bank, "From Green to Sustainable Procurement: It Is Time to Move Ahead!" presentation at International Aid and Trade 2002 conference on "Trade and Development: Building Capacity for Sustainable Markets," New York, 19 June 2002; training from Scot Case, Center for a New American Dream, discussion with author, 13 November 2002.

22. United Nations Environment Programme, "Environmentally & Socially Responsible Procurement," www.sustainableprocurement.net, viewed 17 March 2003.

23. International Council for Local Environmental Initiatives, *Green Purchasing Good Practice Guide* (Freiburg: 2000), p. 31.

24. SWAP (Surplus With a Purpose) website, www.bussvc.wisc.edu/swap.

Index

Other Publications from the Worldwatch Institute

Signposts 2003   NEW!
This CD-ROM provides instant, searchable access to over 1365 pages of full text from the last three editions of *State of the World* and *Vital Signs*, comprehensive datasets going back as far as 50 years, various historical timelines, and easy-to-understand graphs and tables. Fully indexed, *Signposts 2003* contains a powerful search engine for effortless search and retrieval. Plus, it is platform independent and fully compatible with all Windows (3.1 and up), Macintosh, and Unix/Linux operating systems.

Vital Signs 2003   NEW!
Written by Worldwatch's team of researchers, this annual provides comprehensive, user-friendly information on key trends and includes tables and graphs that help readers assess the developments that are changing their lives for better or for worse.

State of the World 2003
Worldwatch's flagship annual is used by government officials, corporate planners, journalists, development specialists, professors, students, and concerned citizens in over 120 countries. Published in more than 20 different languages, it is one of the most widely used resources for analysis.

State of the World Library 2003
Subscribe to the *State of the World Library* and join thousands of decisionmakers and concerned citizens who stay current on emerging environmental issues. The *State of the World Library* includes Worldwatch's flagship annuals, *State of the World* and *Vital Signs*, plus all four of the highly readable, up-to-date, and authoritative *Worldwatch Papers* as they are published throughout the calendar year.

World Watch
This award-winning bimonthly magazine is internationally recognized for the clarity and comprehensiveness of its articles on global trends. Keep up-to-speed on the latest developments in population growth, climate change, species extinction, and the rise of new forms of human behavior and governance.

To make a tax-deductible contribution or to order any of Worldwatch's publications, call us toll-free at 888-544-2303 (or 570-320-2076 outside the U.S.), fax us at 570-322-2063, e-mail us at wwpub@worldwatch.org, or visit our website at www.worldwatch.org.